Photo on title page: What is believed to be a replica of the Nauvoo Temple Angel Moroni still watches over downtown Cincinnati on the top of the Salem Evangelical Church on the corner of Sycamore and Liberty.

Contents

Preface   *v*

CHAPTER 1

A Field White Already to Harvest (1830-1840)   *1*

The First Missionaries Arrive   **2**
The First Converts Join   **11**
The First Branches Are Established   **19**

CHAPTER 2

A Way Station to the West (1840-1890)   *21*

Cincinnati Hosts Regional Conferences   **22**
Local Firms Supply Printing Materials   **27**
Cincinnati Printers Publish Church Books   **33**
Local Newspapers Print Articles on the Church   **35**
The Queen City Entertains Apostates   **40**
Cincinnati Becomes a Temporary Place of Gathering   **41**
An Angel Moroni Comes to Cincinnati   **42**

CHAPTER 3

A Permanent Branch (1890-1935)   *45*

Missionaries Return   **46**
Charles Anderson Establishes a Branch   **50**
The Branch Flourishes   **54**
Church Leaders Visit the Branch   **60**
The Andersons Leave   **63**

CHAPTER 4

A Pillar of the District (1935-1958)   *65*

The Branch Moves On   **65**
Marion Hanks Serves in Cincinnati   **68**
The Branch Renovates a Synagogue   **71**
Creed Haymond Becomes Mission President   **75**
The Branch Helps Lead the District   **76**
The Branch Builds a Chapel   **79**

CHAPTER 5   *The First Modern Stake in Ohio (1958-1985)*   *81*

The District Prepares for Stakehood   **81**
The Cincinnati Stake Is Created   **83**
Blair Evans Establishes the Foundation   **85**
John A. Taylor Educates the Saints   **91**
Joe Banks Lengthens the Stake's Stride   **97**
Robert D. Scott Prepares the Saints   **100**
Wm. Budge Wallis Divides the Stake   **102**

Epilogue   *105*

References   *107*

Index   *111*

Preface

About a year before the Cincinnati Ohio Stake was divided and the Cincinnati Ohio North Stake was created, I felt someone should pull together a history of the LDS Church in the Cincinnati area. I was the stake president at the time, and I asked Stan and Judy Fish to handle this assignment since they were personally acquainted with LDS history in this area. They graciously accepted and began researching and gathering materials.

During a summer vacation they spent several days in the Church Historical Library in Salt Lake City looking up references to Cincinnati in published books, journals, and diaries. They also pulled together a number of short written histories of the Church in Cincinnati. Their research provided the core material for this book. Tom Williams, a son-in-law of Stan and Judy, also spent countless hours on the development and writing of the research. Although Brother and Sister Fish made steady progress, their assignment took more time than expected and years passed with the history far from being completed.

When I was released as stake president in 1990, the new stake president, Brent Somers, gave me the assignment to complete the history. Although some work was done over the next several years, it was not until Brad Kramer volunteered to help that progress moved steadily forward. Brad has unearthed fascinating material that may surprise those who have lived here many years and inspire those unfamiliar with the history of this area. He has conducted interviews with those who were involved with the Church in Cincinnati as it grew from infancy during the first half of this century. He has edited, organized, designed, rewritten, and typeset this book.

Over the years Anne Slater has also been involved in this project. She has reviewed many drafts of each chapter and asked numerous questions, which forced us to dig deeper to provide more detail. She has also patiently copyedited the manuscript numerous times. I think it is fair to say this project would never have been completed without her conscientious and generous contribution.

Thanks also go to many others who have contributed including Chris Bang, Paul Bang, John Harrington, Marie Knott, Alma Ryan, Ruby Steele, Milton Taylor, Tyler Wallis, Brittney Wallis, and Wayne Wilkinson without whom this history would never have been published in the form it is in.

Wm. Budge Wallis, 1997

CHAPTER 1

A Field White Already to Harvest (1830-1840)

by Bradley J. Kramer

And from thence let my servants, Sidney Rigdon, Joseph Smith, Jun., and Oliver Cowdery, take their journey for Cincinnati; And in this place let them lift up their voice and declare my word with loud voices, without wrath or doubting, lifting up holy hands upon them. (Doctrine & Covenants 60:6-7)

Almost as soon as it was organized on April 6, 1830, the Church of Jesus Christ of Latter-day Saints, or the Mormon Church as it is called, has taken a special interest in Cincinnati. This interest was only natural. Headquartered as it quickly was in Kirtland, Ohio, near Cleveland, the Mormon Church early on sent out missionaries "into the regions round about."[1] Soon, as Davis Bitton states, Ohio was filled with Mormon missionaries: "From 1831 to 1837 no state received the 'saturation' treatment that Ohio did. Over and over again it was crisscrossed by Mormon elders on their way or returning from other states."[2]

But even with this general concern, Cincinnati was special. Not only was it prominent on the path west—to Jackson County, Missouri, the next headquarters for the Church—but, in the 1830s and 1840s Cincinnati was becoming the New York City of its region—a bustling, up-and-coming metropolis of commerce and culture.

---

1. Doctrine and Covenants 44:3 (hereafter referred to as D&C).

2. Davis Bitton, "Kirtland as a Center of Missionary Activity, 1830-1838," *BYU Studies* Vol. 11 (Summer 1971): 499.

As Daniel Aaron in his book *Cincinnati, Queen City of the West* writes:

> The easterner, mingling with the crowds in the Cincinnati streets and observing the handsome buildings, could forget the "nursery slanders about backwoods and boors." A compactly built city stood where before had been merely another Ohio river clearing. The quay, paved with limestone and extending three hundred yards along the river, was jammed during the busy seasons of the year; drays and wagons of every kind brought passengers and freight to and from the landing where steamboats arrived and departed hourly. Overlooking the lower level of the city stood rows of rectangular blocks of houses, occasionally relieved by the gilded spires of the churches, and a few conspicuous mansions of the rich. Clouds of smoke poured from chimneys of the Queen City's steam foundries, and behind the city rose the hills, hazy and indistinct, revealing a few houses on their wooded summits.[3]

Despite the fact that W.W. Phelps would later call Cincinnati "a thriving place, as large as Albany but not so handsome,"[4] early missionaries must have seen Cincinnati as an excellent source of large congregations of converts. With an 1830 population of 24,831 (as compared to 1,076 for Cleveland or 2,435 for Columbus),[5] Cincinnati was easily the largest city in Ohio, and it favored religion. As Aaron continues, "Although the riffraff had come with the pious, the majority of the population, as the welter of sects and denominations clearly testify, were a churchgoing if not a spiritual people."[6] Certainly the missionaries would have their troubles, presenting as they were doctrine that was extremely challenging to the usually accepted ideas of the day, but to them Cincinnati must have seemed like an especially promising field of labor, in fact a field "white already to harvest."

The First Missionaries Arrive

Not only were Sidney Rigdon, Joseph Smith, and Oliver Cowdery, three of the most prominent leaders in the early Mormon Church, called to labor in Cincinnati, but so were others including Parley P. Pratt, Peter Whitmer, Ziba Peterson, W.W. Phelps, Lyman Wight, Orson Pratt, Wilford Woodruff, and Orson Hyde. Starting in December 1830, Mormon missionaries have endeavored, despite occasional setbacks and misunderstandings, to share the message of the Mormonism with the good citizens of Cincinnati on a regular, nearly continuous basis.

Sidney Rigdon

3. Daniel Aaron, *Cincinnati, Queen City of the West, 1819-1838* (Columbus: Ohio: Ohio State University Press, 1992), 17.

4. W.W. Phelps, letter to the *Ontario Phoenix* (Canandaigua, New York),7 Sept. 1831.

5. *U.S., Fifth Census: or, Enumeration of the Inhabitants of the United States, As Corrected at the Department of State, 1830* (Washington, D.C.: Duff Green, 1832), 118-43.

6. Aaron, *Cincinnati, Queen City*, 171.

Parley P. Pratt

The "Lamanite" Missionaries

Despite its appeal, Cincinnati did not always greet these Mormon missionaries warmly. Parley P. Pratt, Oliver Cowdery, Peter Whitmer, and Ziba Peterson—probably the first Mormon missionaries to labor in the Cincinnati area—seemed almost discouraged by the lack of interest they generated. Armed with the enthusiasm and vigor of youth, these men arrived in Cincinnati on foot as part of the famous Lamanite Mission. They were traveling west from Kirtland, preaching to the American Indians as they went, with Independence, Missouri, as their final destination. They had just spent several days near Sandusky among the Wyandots. In his autobiography, Parley recorded the following:

> Taking an affectionate leave of [the Wyandots], we continued our journey to Cincinnati. In this city we spent several days, and preached to many of the people, but without much success. About the 20th of December we took passage on a steamer for St. Louis.[7]

Joseph Smith

Joseph Smith himself did not fare better. Together with Emma Smith, Sidney Rigdon, Martin Harris, Edward Partridge, W.W. Phelps, Joseph Coe, and Algernon S. Gilbert passed through Cincinnati on their way to Missouri. Joseph Smith took the occasion to discuss the Church with Walter Scott, a leader of the Campbellites in the area and a former colleague of Sidney Rigdon. On June 19, 1831, the Prophet recorded the following:

Joseph Smith, Jr.

> We went by wagon, canal boats, and stage to Cincinnati where I had an interview with the Reverend Walter Scott, one of the founders of the Campbellites, or New Light Church. Before the close of our interview, he manifested one of the bitterest spirits against the doctrines of the New Testament (that these signs shall follow them that believe) that I have ever witnessed among men. We left Cincinnati in a steamer and landed in Louisville, Kentucky, where we were detained three days in waiting for a steamer to convey us to St. Louis.[8]

That Reverend Scott would not agree with Joseph Smith is not particularly surprising. Although the Campbellites also believed in a general apostasy from Christianity that necessitated "the restoration of the ancient order of things," they did not concur with the idea of modern revelation. In a letter to Sidney Rigdon, who once was a Campbellite preacher, Thomas Campbell declared that the Campbellite faith rested on "the all-sufficiency and the alone-sufficiency of the Holy Scriptures."[9] As Richard Bushman states in *Joseph Smith and the Beginnings of Mormonism*, the Campbellites felt "Joseph Smith went too far when he sought to restore not just the teachings but the methods of the New Testament. Campbell believed Christians were to follow the apostles and prophets, not to be apostles and prophets."[10]

---

7. *Autobiography of Parley P. Pratt* (Salt Lake City, Utah: Deseret Book Company, 1938), 51.

8. Joseph Smith, Jr., *History of the Church of Jesus Christ of Latter-day Saints,* ed. B.H. Roberts (Salt Lake City, Utah: Church of Jesus Christ of Latter-day Saints, 1932-51) 1:188.

9. A.S. Hayden, *Early History of the Disciples in the Western Reserve, Ohio* (Cincinnati: Chase and Hall, 1875; reprinted, New York: Arno Press and the New York Times, 1972), 218.

Walter Scott

Frustrating as this interview was, at least it was better than the experience Joseph Smith had a year later, in April 1832. At that time, he had just been run out of Kirtland by a mob, after having been tarred, feathered, and beaten. Unfortunately, the mob followed him to Cincinnati:

> After we left Hiram, fearing for the safety of my family on the account of the mob, I wrote to my wife (in connection with Bishop Whitney) suggesting that she go to Kirtland and tarry with Brother Whitney's family until our return. From Wheeling we took passage on board the steamer Trenton. While at dock during the night, the boat was twice on fire, burning the whole width of the boat through into the cabin, but with so little damage that the boat went on in the morning; and when we arrived at Cincinnati, some of the mob had followed us, left us, and we arrived in Louisville the same night. Captain Brittle offered us protection on board his boat and gave us supper and breakfast gratuitously.[11]

Lyman Wight and Calves Wilson

In time other missionaries began to make headway. Lyman Wight, who later became a member of the Council of the Twelve, stopped in Cincinnati later in 1831. He and Calves Wilson, Lyman Wight's companion, were greeted with a more encouraging reception, in spite of, or perhaps because of, Lyman's unorthodox style:

> [Lyman Wight] went to Cincinnati on a mission to preach the gospel. On arriving in that city he called at a hotel and engaged his board for several weeks. The landlord asked him what his business was. He replied he was a preacher of the gospel after the order of Melchisedek [sic]. He created so much curiosity that they wished to hear him preach. He told them that was his business, and if they would open the court house he would do so willingly. They obtained the house, and he delivered a series of lectures and built up a branch of the Church, and baptized upwards of one hundred. The family of Higbees were among the first baptized; they were fishermen, and Wight would fish with them through the day and preach at night. One evening he went from the fish net to the court house, and stood on top of a stove barefooted with his trousers rolled up his knees, and his shirt sleeves up to his elbows, and preached two hours. Some of the people remarked, "He preaches the truth, though he does not look much like a preacher."[12]

Apparently, many were able to look beyond Lyman Wight's appearance. He and Calvis Wilson baptized approximately a hundred and established the first branch of the Church in Cincinnati. In the words of Orange Wight, Lyman's son:

> [Lyman Wight] went on a mission to Cincinnati, Ohio about the last of the year 1831. Father raised up a large branch at Cincinnati, many of which came to Jackson County during the year 1832.[13]

10. Richard Bushman, *Joseph Smith and the Beginnings of Mormonism* (Urbana and Chicago: University of Illinois Press, 1984), 183.

11. Smith, *History of the Church,* 1:266.

12. Andrew Jenson, *Latter-day Saint Biographical Encyclopedia* (Salt Lake City, Utah: Andrew Jenson History Company, 1910, reprinted, Salt Lake City, Utah: Western Epics), 1:93-94.

Orson Pratt and Lorenzo D. Barnes

If Lyman Wight was Cincinnati's most colorful missionary, Orson Pratt, the brother of Parley P. Pratt, was its most dedicated, certainly the most widely traveled. Orson—who later became an apostle, writer, and well-known defender of Mormonism—came to the Cincinnati area in the winter of 1835. He came with Lorenzo D. Barnes, a man who, though born with a speech impediment and not blessed with much education, eventually became a fine speaker and missionary. Together, Lorenzo and Orson preached in Covington, Kentucky, and Brookville, Indiana, as well as in several southwestern Ohio cities and villages, including downtown Cincinnati, Harrison, Cummingsville, Newtown, Batavia, Mulberry, Perintown, and Milford.

Orson Pratt

At that time, Orson Pratt was returning to Kirtland from Missouri. He had been part of the epic march of Zion's Camp and although Zion's Camp did not rescue the Mormons in Missouri from oppression, Orson felt that "the promises of the Lord were verified . . . we were blessed and counseled from on high throughout the journey."[14] He left Missouri on August 21, 1834, in the company of his brother William Dickinson Pratt. Orson had served in the high council in Missouri for six months previous and had determined to preach his way back to Kirtland, trusting in the Lord to provide for himself and William. His resolve was quickly challenged as they traveled along the Missouri River to Illinois. Orson, who was still fighting off cholera, suffered fever and convulsions on and off for months. As he wrote in his journal, he sometimes "lay down upon the wet prairies, many miles from any house, being unable to travel."

William left his brother at Vandalia, Illinois, and Orson, despite his illness, continued on alone, preaching as he went, to Terre Haute. There Orson baptized two converts and joined John Murdock, another Mormon missionary on his way to Kirtland. In Sugar Creek, Indiana, they met two more Mormon missionaries, Lorenzo D. Barnes and Lewis Robbins, who had been preaching and baptizing in Shelbyville. After "holding a few meetings in this region, and baptizing a few," Elders Murdock and Robbins decided to go directly to Kirtland while Elders Pratt and Barnes opted to first visit Cincinnati, again preaching as they traveled.

As Lorenzo D. Barnes wrote in his journal:

> We . . . proseded towards Cincinnati on Saturday and Sunday evenings being the 3rd & 4th (of April, 1835) held meetings in a small village in Rush Co. called Salem We laid before the people the ancient order of things and the great work to be brought about in the Last days according to the Prophecies of the old and New Testaments The people listened with great attention & much of their prejudices appeared to be remooved . . . on the 17th arived at the village of Brookville at 4 pm and held meeting in the court house in the evening and one on the next day at 2 00 pm it being the Sabath After preaching had quite a debate with a Universalian

13. Recollections of Orange L. Wight, son of Lyman Wight, typescript, BYU. Bunkerville, Nevada, May 4, 1903.

14. Breck England, *The Life and Thought of Orson Pratt* (Salt Lake City, Utah: University of Utah Press, 1985), 36.

preacher by the name of St Johns Monday evening the 19th held meeting in the village of Harison . . . laid before them the ancient gospel . . . the hearts of many of the people were stired up and numbers were led to seek seriously & diligently to know whether these teachings were so or not The priests of the day used there greatest exertions to put down the Truth but all they could do was to read Newspaper stories call for signs and cry fals[e] prophet fals[e] teacher delusion imposition &c but this was but little affect on the minds of those had herd the doctrine and were honest . . . our manner of teaching the people generly was—in the first place to lay before them the first principles of the gospel faith repentance Baptism for the remission of sins & the laying on of the hands for the gift of the holy ghost these we proved from the New testament to the people were preached and practiced by he Apostles and obeyed by the people in ancient days and Paul says if we or an Angel from heaven preach any other let him be accursed and then by comparring the ancient order of things with the teachings of the preasant generation and left the people to judge who were denying it proved the nesesity of more revelations where ever the church of Christ is on the earth and then that according to the prophecies there will be more revelations given in the last days to bring about the great work that is to be accomplished And then the prophecies concerning the restoration of the hous[e] of Israel and the means that God will make us[e] of to bring about the great work The covenants made to the Fathers the Comeing of Chris[t] his kingdom and reign on the Earth &c &c.[sic][15]

The good people of Brookville, Indiana, were quite impressed. According to the *Brookville Enquirer:*

On last Saturday evening, for the first time, in this place, a gentleman, and minister belonging to this new sect [the Mormons], preached in the courthouse, to a very respectable audience; and discoursed briefly on the various subjects connected with his creed; explained his faith and gave a brief history of the Book of Mormon—united it with the Holy Bible, etc.

By request, he tarried over Sabbath, and at 2 o'clock again opened public worship by an able address to the throne of the Most High. He spoke for about an hour and a half to a very large audience, during which time he explained many important passages of the prophecies contained in the Old and New Testaments, and applied them according to their literal meaning. He was not lame in the attempt, and in a succinct and lucid manner imparted his belief to the audience.

He believes the Book of Mormon to be a series of revelations, and other matters appertaining to the Ephraimites, Lamanites, etc., whom he believes to have been the original settlers of this continent; and that an ancient prophet caused the plates from which the Book of Mormon was translated to be buried nearly two thousand years ago, in what is now called Ontario County; New York. He is also of the belief that Joseph Smith was cited to the plates by an angel from heaven, and endowed with the gift to translate the engraving upon them into the known language of the country.

15. Lorenzo Dow Barnes, Diary, 2 vols., Church Archives, Historical Department, Church of Jesus Christ of Latter-day Saints, Salt Lake City, Utah, 1:7-9.

This book, he is of opinion, is an event intended to prepare for the great work, the second appearance of Christ, when he shall stand on the Mount of Olives, attended by Abraham and all the Saints, to reign on the earth for the space of a thousand years.

After he had closed his discourse, on Sabbath afternoon, he remarked that if "no one had anything to say, the meeting would be considered as closed." Reverend Daniel St. John, a clergyman of the universal order, ascended the pulpit and in his usual eloquent strain held forth for a considerable time; taking exceptions to some of the positions of the preceding speaker—more particularly as regarded his belief as to the second appearance of Christ, and his doctrine of future rewards and punishments. An interesting debate of about three hours ensued in which each had four hearings, and at the request of the audience, a division of the house was called for on the merits of the argument, and carried in favor of the Latter-day Saint by an overwhelming vote.

Though in some things he characterized the fanatic; yet, in the main, his doctrines were sound and his positions tenable. We would do injustice to the gentleman were we to omit stating, that in all the discourses, of the like character, that we have ever heard it has never fallen to our lot to hear so much harmony in the arrangement of quotations from the sacred book. No passage could be referred to that would in the least produce discord in his arguments. The whole of his discourses were delivered in a very clear and concise manner, rendering it obvious that he was thoroughly acquainted with the course he believed he was called upon to pursue, in obedience to his Master's will.

If a man may be called eloquent who transfers his own views and feelings into the breasts of others—if a knowledge of the subject, and to speak without fear—are a part of the more elevated rules of eloquence, we have no hesitancy in saying ORSON PRATT was eloquent; and truly verified the language of Boileau: "What we clearly conceive, we can clearly express."[16]

On Tuesday, January 20, as Orson wrote in his journal, they "[c]rossed the Ohio River, visited a small branch of the Church on Licking River [in Kentucky], tarried with them two weeks, preaching almost every evening."[17] This small branch had been built up by Robert Culbertson, a convert from Sugar Creek, Shelby county, Indiana, who had moved to Kentucky in 1834.[18] Orson later wrote that he had baptized "seven in Campbell County, Kentucky, eight miles from Cincinnati: the church in that place now numbers eighteen."[19]

---

16. "Mormons," *Messenger & Advocate*, Oliver Cowdery ed. (Feb 1835), 1:77.

17. *The Orson Pratt Journals*, comp. Elden J. Watson (Salt Lake City, Utah: Elden Jay Watson, 1975), 7.

18. Andrew Jenson, *Encyclopedic History of The Church of Jesus Christ of Latter-day Saints* (Salt Lake City, Utah: Deseret News Publishing Company, 1941), 397.

19. *Orson Pratt Journals*, 7.

On February 6, Elders Pratt and Barnes left Kentucky and returned to Cincinnati and began preaching in the city and nearby towns. As Orson recorded in his journal:

> February 6, 1835. Left the small church on Licking River in Kentucky and came to Cincinnati and called on Brother Morrison with a determination to preach in the city if a house could be obtained with little difficulty. Brother Morrison obtained a large and commodious schoolhouse situated on the corner of Vine and Sixth Streets by paying $1.00 per night for the use of the same with firewood and light.
>
> February 12th. On Thursday evening we appointed a meeting and gave general notice to several congregations. Thursday evening came and a large congregation assembled and we laid before them the order of the ancient gospel. The people listened with great attention. We left another appointment in the same house for the next week on Friday evening. [20]

After preaching in Fulton, an area on the banks of the Ohio River roughly between the present-day 471 bridge and Torrance Avenue, at the house of a Sister Muttings, Elders Pratt and Barnes kept their return appointment in Cincinnati, preaching on "the scattering and gathering of the house of Israel and the great manifestation of the power of God which will be shown forth at the time of their restoration." They then arranged for another appointment there for the next Tuesday evening. During this third appointment, Orson again addressed restoration topics, preaching "the means which God would use for the restoration of the house of Israel" and "something about the blessings which were given to the tribe of Joseph and also the 29th chapter of Isaiah."

All in all, Orson Pratt felt that his trip to Cincinnati was very successful. Concerning his time there, Orson Pratt later wrote to Oliver Cowdery:

> [Since February 16] we have preached three times in Cincinnati, three times in Fulton and three times in the village of Cummingsville, six miles from the city. We have had large Congregations and many are astonished at the doctrine; some believe, many disbelieve and others obey. We have this day baptized two [Ann Morrison and Jane Bliven] who reside in Cincinnati. There are now 22 or 23 members of the Church in Fulton and Cincinnati. We expect to leave this place soon for the village of Batavia about 20 miles distant. Brother Barns and myself preached twice in the court house at Brookville, Indiana—we were kindly received by the people of that village, and were solicited to tarry longer, but we could not conveniently: it was the first time the people in that place had heard concerning the principles of our faith, and it was somewhat marvelous to them, perhaps rendered more so in consequence of a short debate which lasted about three or four hours, principally upon the Second Coming of Christ. [21]

---

20. Ibid.

21. *Journal History of the Church of Jesus Christ of Latter-day Saints*, 16 February 1835, Church Archives, Historical Department, Church of Jesus Christ of Latter-day Saints, Salt Lake City.

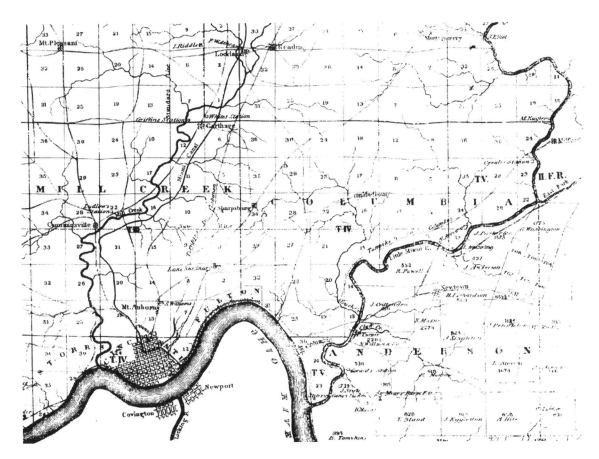

Eastern Hamilton County, 1835

Orson Pratt was a skilled debater. On March 1, he and Elder Barnes, after delivering their own sermons, went to hear a Campbellite minister named L.H. Jameson preach. After the sermon, Orson Pratt challenged the preacher, whom he described as "quite a talented man," to meet him "before the public and enter into an investigation of the subject of spiritual gifts" and said that he "would pledge [himself] to prove from the scriptures that miracles, gifts of healings, prophecies, revelations, and all the spiritual gifts which were in the Church in the days of the Savior and Apostles were necessary for the Church of Christ now, and that there never was nor ever will be a true church on the earth in a state of mortality without them." The minister accepted and they agreed to debate in Carthage, a few miles distant, at the home of a Mr. Walter Scott and Doctor Wright. Mr. Jameson said he would inform Elder Pratt on what day he or another minister would meet him in Carthage. The minister, however, backed out of the publicly agreed upon appointment, much to his embarrassment. Such confrontations, apparently, were frequent.

On March 6, 1835, Elders Pratt and Barnes took their leave of Cincinnati and traveled eastward, probably following the Ohio River along present-day Eastern Avenue and then continuing along a road we now call Route 32. That evening they preached in Newtown, then a small village ten miles east of Cincinnati.

They continued east the next day, again following Route 32, journeying to Batavia. They remained there preaching several days, mostly at a schoolhouse owned by a "Methodist man." On March 11, they traveled twelve miles northwest to Newbury (part of present-day Mulberry), Perintown (then called Perrin's Mills), and then to Milford. At Milford they preached at various schoolhouses, including one near John Kugler's store, which was near the present-day Millcroft Inn. They found many willing listeners and stayed in the area nearly two weeks, holding forty meetings and baptizing two persons, including a Margaret Magrew who was baptized in the Little Miami River. On April 20, 1835, they left for Kirtland.

On the whole, Orson Pratt's missionary tour of the Cincinnati area was amazing. Although they converted only a handful, they covered a large area and an astoundingly wide variety of topics, including: the falling away of the church, the losing of their authority to administer ordinances, the restoration of the church or gospel according to John's revelations, spiritual gifts, the Second Coming of Christ, the first principles of the gospel, the coming forth of the Book of Mormon, the scattering and gathering of Israel, the new covenant with Israel in the last days, the gathering of the Jews in unbelief, the gathering of Saints to Zion, the blessings pronounced upon the tribe of Joseph, a history of the Book of Mormon, the two sticks and the blessings on Joseph, a short history of the prophecies that had been fulfilled, the reign of the Saints on the earth for a thousand years, the difference between faith and knowledge, and finally the fruits of the kingdom among the Jews and also among Gentiles.

And Elder Pratt's later quality of sermons was also evident. The people of Brookville were so impressed with the Mormon missionaries they wrote them a letter requesting they return:

> Sir: there is a general wish through this country, that you would call and give us another hearing when opportunity will permit—send us a letter and we will give public notice when you will attend; and we have no hesitation in saying, that you will be heard by the largest congregation ever assembled in this country. Your expenses during your stay, will be defrayed.
>
> Yours respectfully.
> (signed) Edit's of Brookville Inquirer."[22]

After Orson Pratt, missionaries continued to flow into the Cincinnati area. Unfortunately, few events in the area for some time were recorded. There are references to elders being in southern Ohio but little detail. On September 23, 1840, Elder John E. Page—then a member of the Council of

22. Orson Pratt, letter to editor, *Messenger & Advocate*, March 1835, Oliver Cowdery ed., 89-90.

the Twelve—came to Cincinnati and, according to Samuel Bent, preached "with the manefestations [sic] of the Spirit and power in [Cincinnati]." During his stay, he claimed to have baptized thirteen converts here. [23]

The First Converts Join

Unlike the missionaries who labored here, little is known about the many people who first joined the Church in Cincinnati. They were most probably common folk who left little notice of their comings and goings. Three notable exceptions are the Higbee family, David Pettegrew, and Martha Jane Knowlton.

The Higbee Family

Isaac Higbee, the father of Elias and Isaac, Jr., was a religious, enterprising, not particularly well educated farmer. In 1803, he, then a confirmed Methodist, had just arrived in the Cincinnati area with his young family. Isaac Higbee had followed the Reverend John Collins across the Alleghenies from New Jersey. Reverend Collins, later known as "Old Man Eloquent of the M.E. Church," had heard of the economic potential of the Cincinnati area and had traveled to Columbia, Ohio, the previous year to look it over for the possibility of settlement. He was very impressed with what he saw and chose a tract of land on East Fork, near Batavia.

This tract, called "Horseshoe Bottoms," was well known for its many sugar maples (still bearing the blazes cut by Indians), dependable springs (including a salt spring known as "Elk Lick"), and fast-flowing creeks and streams, which could be used to power mills. It must have seemed to Reverend Collins like a perfect place to settle.

The next spring Isaac Higbee along with Reverend Collins, Cornelius McCullum, and Edward Doughty bought the land from General William Lytle. Later they brought with twelve to fifteen families with them across the Alleghenies to Pittsburgh where they then bought a large boat and floated down the Ohio River to their new home. Once there they quickly cleared the land, put in crops, built cabins, and established a church. Reverend Collins preached the first Methodist sermon in the Cincinnati area in 1804 and donated a lot for a log cabin meetinghouse, which was known as Collins' chapel. In 1818 a larger chapel was built for the growing congregation and was dubbed the Bethel Church.

The Bethel Church quickly became the heart of the growing community but eventually burned down. However, in 1867 it was rebuilt and this time was called the Old Bethel Methodist Episcopal Church. This edifice can still be seen in Bantam along with a small cemetery where Reverend Collins, his family, several Higbee children (James C., Elmira, and A.V.H.), and Ulysses S. Grant's grandparents are buried. The strong stone home Isaac Higbee built as evidence of his commitment to the area stood for over 160 years (during part of which it may have been used in the Underground Railroad) until it

23. Smith, *History of the Church*, 4:199.

was taken down for preservation. Unfortunately, Isaac's home has not yet been reconstructed and its interior woodwork, which was said to be exquisite, may have been destroyed in a fire. However, according to records, it was a fine home and bore the initials IH for Isaac Higbee and SH for Sophia Higbee, his wife, as well as the date of its construction on its cornerstone.

Given this obvious commitment, it is puzzling why the Higbees moved from their large home to a site closer to Cincinnati. But move they did, probably in 1817. By this time they were a large family, including not only Isaac and Sophia but their three sons (Elias, John S., and Isaac Jr.), their three daughters, and their various in-laws and grandchildren. Together they moved en masse to Lewistown, a small town on the Ohio River, near Cincinnati in an area just west of Torrance Avenue called "The Eastern Liberties" because Cincinnati laws did not apply there. There they fished for a living and later became acquainted with Lyman Wight and heard the message of the Restoration. As John S. Higbee, younger brother to Elias, states:

> John S. Higbee Son of Isaac & Sophia Higbee was Born in tate township Clermont Co. State of Ohio My fathers family consisted of 3 Boys & 3 girls I was the youngest of the family I went to Scool somthing near 5 year at the age of 14 I went to learn the cabinet trade with Peter [O]liver my Brotherinlaw I remained with him about 5 years I then went home to my parents who lived in cincinnati I set in to fishing with a net with my father for a living. . .. I Bought property in Lewistown & Built 2 houses in that place & allso moved there 12 m from there to Portsmouth 100 m from there to same place Back 100 m we Lived in Lewistown State of Ohio Hamilton Co. when we heard the gospel preached By Elders Lyman wight & calvis wilson the first opportunity I had I was Baptized By calvis wilson received the Laying on of the hands for the receiption of the holy ghost by Lyman wight this being about the first of may - 1831 in about the [ ] of [-1832] we sold our possessions for 6 Hundred Dollars & moved to Jackson Co. mo to the place where the Lord had pointed out for the gathering of his Saints[24]

With the Higbees went the entire membership of the Cincinnati Branch, moving to Jackson County in the spring of 1833. Rejoining their original missionary, they relocated on the Big Blue and Round Grove Creek with Lyman Wight.

Elias and Isaac Higbee, Jr. later became quite prominent in the Church—Elias serving as the Church Recorder and a senior county judge in Caldwell County, Missouri; and Isaac heading up a later Mormon effort to colonize the Provo area, thirty miles south of Salt Lake City. John was ordained a bishop in Nauvoo and served a mission in England. He was also in the first pioneer company to reach the Great Salt Lake.

---

24. From an unpublished autobiography of John S. Higbee, Church Archives.

Of the Higbees, Orange Wight said they were "all good men" but seemed particularly grateful for Isaac and John Higbee.

> It was Isaac and John Higbee that helped my mother and I all through the Missouri troubles and when we got to Quincy, Illinois, helped me to make a living for mother and now her five little children, of which I have written, while father was in prison in Missouri.[25]

David Pettegrew

David Pettegrew

David Pettegrew likewise was not born in Cincinnati. He was born in Weatherfield, Vermont, on July 29, 1791, but soon after attaining his adulthood headed west. David, along with his wife, Elizabeth, and his brother Nathan and his family, traveled to Olean, New York, and purchased a boat. They then floated down the Allegheny River to Pittsburgh and from there continued on down the Ohio to Cincinnati, where he became a master Mason (Harmony Lodge, No. 2). A few years later David moved his family just across the Indiana border, somewhere in Dearborn County, where several of his children were born.

According to his journal, David Pettegrew was not born a religious man. His interest in spiritual matters came later:

> I made no profession of religion until the year eighteen hundred and twenty-three when I became much concerned about my own welfare. I mourned and lamented much, for I had sinned against my God, and feared that if I did not change my sinful ways my soul must be lost. I cried much unto the Lord for mercy, but I feared that I had gone beyond redemption, and that I must see and feel the damnation of hell, but through the mercies of the Almighty God, I found rest to my soul. I was now determined to lead a new life, and to serve my God the remainder of my days.[26]

However, once converted, David did his best to do his duty to God and to his fellow men, teaching a Methodist Sunday School and often calling upon his neighbors to "become Christians and pray unto the Lord, with their families, and also in secret." And apparently, not a few of his neighbors followed his advice.

In these efforts as well as his financial pursuits, David felt blessed. The Pettegrews apparently lived comparatively well, having "a good farm, an orchard and many other conveniences for which [he] felt grateful." Nevertheless, David and his family were not without their trials. His daughter, Lydia, for instance, died suddenly for no apparent reason. Characteristically, David rejoiced that "she had gone to her home . . . to await the glorious day when all the just and the faithful will hear the voice of Him who hath authority, and will comfort in the first resurrection."[27]

---

25. Wight, typescript.

26. David Pettegrew, journal, holograph copy, Brigham Young University Special Collections, Provo, Utah. Grammar has been standardized.

27. Ibid.

And so David continued until 1832 when a friend, whom David considered "a just and upright man, but not very intelligent" asked him if he had heard about the Mormons. David responded honestly:

> I replied that I never had only from what I had read in the Christian's Advocate, printed at New York. I there read some slurs about a people that were gathering in the upper part of the state of Missouri, and supposed they were a fit people for the penitentiary. [28]

Unfazed the friend replied that he thought the Mormons were a "good people" and then lent David a copy of the Book of Mormon to read. David was very much intrigued:

> [T]his was indeed new to me, and I thought a trick, as he looked upon this book, as sacred as on the Bible. I opened the book, it was the second book of Nephi, and the fifth chapter. I read on a while my thoughts were very active, what to think I knew not: It was entirely a new thing to me and I began to mind what I was reading, although I observed to my wife that I did not think that it was the words of him that had a devil. [29]

David continued reading The Book of Mormon until it was time to go to his Sunday School class. There David allowed the Mormon missionary to speak and afterward urged all not to dismiss what the man had said:

> [A]fter he had spoken what he saw fit he sat down, and I immediately arose and spoke as follows, brethren there has been certainly strange things come to our ears, that we had not thought of, which is entirely new to us, therefore, I recommend that we be wise and not hasty in making up our minds concerning this matter, for if it is of man, it will be good for nothing and will soon come to naught, but if it should be of God, and we should be found at variance with it, we would be exceedingly sorry in days to come. I know not whether it is of God or of man, but this much I do know, that there is no harm in being wise in these things, and I took my seat. [30]

After the meeting, the missionary left only to return a few weeks later, bringing with him a Book of Mormon that David could buy. This David did and thus brought upon himself censure from the local circuit preacher, Doctor Oglesby. David Pettegrew in return asked Doctor Oglesby to take the Book of Mormon with him on his circuit and read it, noting anything that seemed in conflict with the Bible. Doctor Oglesby accepted the book but did not meet the conditions, claiming that it was "not worth reading." Despite not reading the book, Doctor Oglesby called upon David to "take [his] Book of Mormon and burn it as a sacrifice to old Moloch." David refused and instead resigned his post as a Sunday School teacher as he continued studying The Book of Mormon.

---

28. Ibid.
29. Ibid.
30. Ibid.

The persecution persisted. However, David did not complain:

> These things caused me to draw nearer to the Lord, and he to me and he witnessed to me that he had now began his work for the last days, and that the Book of Mormon was the true book and by it I saw that the Lord was the same Lord, and its gospel was the same and its ordinances were the same as those I had been thought to observe. But man, poor man had changed or transgressed the law, changed the ordinances, and had broken the everlasting covenant, and yet the Lord had spared the earth notwithstanding the many ways, parties, and sects, we had been divided into, and yet none right; but all had gone astray. I truly saw that God was of long suffering and of much patience. My heart was poured out in prayer to my God, and the solemnity of eternity rested upon my mind. . . I, therefore, searched the prophesies and I plainly saw that there was much yet to be fulfilled, and the world was still in the dark regarding this matter, and my heart was pained and weighed down with sorrow because of the gross darkness that covered the minds of the people.[31]

David Pettegrew was soon baptized by Isaac Higbee in Cincinnati later on that year (1832). During the following winter, he left the Cincinnati area for Missouri, only to be driven out of the land he purchased and forced to flee to Nauvoo.

In Nauvoo David served as a captain in the Nauvoo Legion and was present during the laying of the cornerstones of the Nauvoo Temple. He was elected to the high council in Iowa and also served as one of the leaders of the Mormon Battalion during their historic march to California. "Owing to his silver locks and fatherly counsels," David was known as Father Pettegrew, the patriarch and chaplain of the battalion.[32] Battalion members often turned to him for sympathy and advice. In Utah David was elected a senator in the Provisional State of Deseret, and served as chaplain in the lower house of the Utah legislature during the sessions of 1857-58 and 1860-61. He was called as Bishop of the 10th Ward, Salt Lake City, in April 1849 and later served as an assistant presiding bishop in 1852.

One particularly poignant moment in David's life came in 1844 when he was called on a mission to New York and was able to visit his former friends in the Cincinnati area. There he clearly demonstrated his ability to speak his mind even sharply and still retain the goodwill and friendship of others:

> From Kirtland I went to Indiana, Dearborn county, my old place of residence. My neighbors received me cordially; they opened the Baptist meeting house on the Sabbath, which was crowded with people. I felt to call on the Lord in their behalf. I had liberty in speaking from the prophets and showing the literal gathering of the house of Israel, and their restoration to the lands of their fathers. In the evening in holding forth the Book of Mormon, the spirit of the Lord was there in great power. I could have held a protracted meeting, but I had a number of appointments to fill a distance from there. I therefore took the parting hand with my old

---

31. Ibid.

32. B.H. Roberts, A *Comprehensive History of the Church of Jesus Christ of Latter-day Saints* (Salt Lake City, Utah: Church of Jesus Christ of Latter-day Saints, 1957), 3: 114.

neighbors. They gave me three dollars and said remember us and call again as soon as consistent, they owned me as a friend. I passed on to Franklin and Fayette counties, where I had good success among the people until the conference at Trenton, November 16, and 17th, which was an interesting time; I then took leave of our brethren for Nauvoo.[33]

David Pettegrew died on the 30th of December, 1863, at Salt Lake City.

Martha Jane Knowlton

Martha Jane Knowlton

Unlike the Higbees and David Pettegrew, Martha Jane Knowlton was born in the Cincinnati area but joined the Church elsewhere. The fourth of ten children, she was born in Covington, Kentucky, in 1822, her family having recently moved from Boone County. In 1827 they moved across the Ohio to Cumminsville and remained there until 1835 when they packed up again for Hancock County, Illinois. Martha's father, Sidney, raised cattle there and was quickly known in the area as a "scientific farmer."

During the winter of 1838-39, many Latter-day Saints came into Hancock County, where Nauvoo would be established, as they fled the persecution in Missouri. As devout Campbellites Martha and her family took pity on these people and felt it was their Christian duty to help them. It was at this time that the Knowltons first became acquainted with the doctrines of the Restored Gospel and, although they were so knowledgeable that their missionaries, George A. Smith and John E. Page, thought at times that they were discussing the Gospel with Thomas Campbell himself, they quickly embraced it. According to family tradition the Knowltons were baptized through a hole cut in the ice of the Mississippi in January or February 1840. A few months later Martha met Howard Coray, her future husband, after a Church meeting.

Howard Coray was a well-educated Latter-day Saint and personal friend of Joseph Smith, having been his clerk for a time and also helping him begin a history of the church. At a church meeting, 23-year-old Howard noticed a striking, 18-year-old woman with "dark brown eyes, very bright and penetrating" sitting in a buggy. After the meeting, Howard decided to go for a walk, and, as he stated in his journal, "see what [he] could see." He did not have to walk long:

> I had not gone far before I came square in front of the lovely miss, walking arm in arm with a Mrs. Harris, with whom I was well acquainted. They stopped and Mrs. Harris said, "Brother Coray, I have the honor of introducing you to Miss Martha Knowlton, from Bear Creek. I, of course, bowed as politely as I knew how and she curtsied, and we then fell into somewhat familiar conversation. I discovered at once that she was ready, off hand, and inclined to be witty; also, that her mind took a wider range than was common for young ladies of her age. This interview, though short, was indeed very enjoyable, and closed with the hope that she might be the one whom the Lord had picked for me; and thus it proved to be.[34]

33. David Pettegrew, "Communications," *Times and Seasons,* 21 Dec. 1844, 5:765-766.

34. Howard Coray Journal, typescript, Brigham Young University Archives and Manuscripts, Provo, Utah, 11-12.

Howard Coray did not go into the intimate details of their courtship in his journal. However, he did note that he showed a letter he had written to her to his friend Joseph Smith. According to Brother Coray, Joseph Smith immediately took an "uncommon interest in the matter and took pains to see her and talk with her about [him]."[35] Apparently Joseph approved, becoming a kind of matchmaker for them. They were married in Martha's family home in Bear Creek on 6 February 1841 by Robert B. Thompson.

Martha immediately joined her new husband in his work as a schoolteacher. Although largely self-taught, Martha was said to be quite accomplished. As her daughter, Martha Jane Knowlton Coray Lewis, wrote:

> {Martha was] a rapid and lucid writer, a brilliant conversationalist, and a fine speaker on a wide range of subjects. She had a fair knowledge of law, philosophy, history, poetry, chemistry and geology—the latter two being her favorite studies. She could and did assay minerals, and distil herbs, write eloquent lectures, and cook dinners that would tempt the appetite of an epicure." [36]

According to Charles Tate, Martha and Howard worked from the beginning "as a matched team. It did not matter which one needed assistance, the other would pitch in and help. Each found happiness in the other's success."[37] She took quickly to teaching, working side by side with her husband, and taught, among others, the Smith children.

In addition to teaching, Martha excelled at writing. Soon after her baptism, she came to know and greatly admire Joseph Smith as a prophet of God. She took it upon herself to write down every discourse he ever delivered. Church Historian George A. Smith noted that she was more diligent in preserving the Prophet's sayings than any other woman in the Church.[38] Not only did she record Joseph Smith's speeches, but she apparently carried a pencil and paper to every church meeting she attended in order to write down what was said. Noting this habit, Lucy Mack Smith, Joseph Smith's mother, chose Martha as her scribe to whom she dictated her history of her son. Howard Coray became involved later on in this project, but essentially *History of Joseph Smith by his Mother, Lucy Mack Smith* was all written down by Martha.

In addition to her teaching and writing work, Martha served in the original Relief Society in Nauvoo and was appointed secretary to the first Relief Society in Salt Lake City. So accomplished was Martha that later on, after the exodus west when Brigham Young was forming Brigham Young Academy, which later became Brigham Young University, he appointed Martha to the three-member Board of Trustees "to represent women's interests."[39] Martha did this as well as representing the interests of the Church at large.

---

35. Ibid, 12.

36. Martha J.C. Lewis, "Martha J. Knowlton Coray," *Improvement Era*, 5 (April 1902):440.

37. Charles D. Tate, Jr.,"Howard and Martha Jane Knowlton Coray of Nauvoo," *Regional Studies--Illinois*, ed. H. Dean Garrett (Provo, Utah: Department of Church History and Doctrine, Brigham Young University, 1995), 339.

38. Dean C. Jessee, "Joseph Smith's 19 July 1840 Discourse," *BYU Studies*, 19 (Spring 1979): 390.

39. Tate, "Howard and Martha Jane Knowlton Coray," 349-50.

In a letter to Brigham Young, Martha noted that for her:

> [the] principle of education has been God's laws of religion first, Man's laws of honor and morality second, Science of every attainable kind [next]. Does not the Deed [of Brigham Young Academy] require the sacred book[s] mentioned [the Bible, Book of Mormon, and Doctrine and Covenants] to be taken up as a study in the same way as the sciences mentioned?[40]

Generations of BYU graduates very possibly owe their religious training to Martha Jane Knowlton.

In addition to serving on the board of trustees, Martha also wrote articles for the *Territorial Enquirer* (the Provo newspaper) and contributed to *The Woman's Exponent.* Brigham Young University later recognized Martha's contribution to the early development of the university by naming the assembly room in the newly remodeled Karl G. Maeser Building the Martha Jane Knowlton Coray Lecture Hall.

When Martha died, an obituary in *The Salt Lake Herald* wrote that Mrs. Coray "was a remarkable woman and her superior qualities impressed themselves upon those who approached her even for a brief period. She was possessed of indomitable energy, and [she was] widely read and cultured."[41] *The Deseret News* added that she was "a woman among ten thousand . . . Almost by her own exertion she reared a family of twelve children . . . She possessed a great independence of character, marked natural intelligence and considerable culture. The nobler traits of womankind have been exhibited in her life to a degree that is seldom excelled." [42]

In his journal, Howard Coray recalled a prophecy Joseph Smith had made concerning him during his early years. "Bro. Coray," Joseph said, "you will soon find a companion, one that will be suited to your condition, and whom you will be satisfied with. She will cling to you, like the cords of death; and you will have a good many children."[43] Howard Corey, later in life, testified that this prophecy had been clearly fulfilled:

> I will say in this connection that what the Prophet said in regard to the companion which I should soon find has been fully verified. A more intelligent, self-sacrificing, and devoted wife and mother, few men have been blessed with. She became the mother of twelve children, seven sons and five daughters, and lived to see them all grown up to man and womanhood, educated, intelligent, virtuous and religious. In this great work, she acted well her part.[44]

No finer tribute could be given for this woman from Covington.

40. Martha Jane Knowlton Coray to Brigham Young, Brigham Young Papers, Church Archives, Church of Jesus Christ of Latter-day Saints, Salt Lake City, Utah.

41. Obituary, "Martha Jane Knowlton Coray," *Salt Lake Herald*, 16 December 1881.

42. Obituary, "Martha Jane Knowlton Coray," *Deseret News*, 21 December 1881.

43. Coray Journal, 9.

44. Ibid, 11.

James Burch

Others

In addition to those already mentioned, other native Cincinnatians contributed greatly to the building up of the Latter-day Saint Church. Riley Garner Clark, born July 29, 1829 in Cincinnati, joined the Church in Martinsville, Ohio, and later enlisted with the Mormon Battalion. After he arrived in Utah, Brigham Young called him to set up a tannery and shoe shop in Manti, Utah. He later did the same in Panguitch, Utah.[45] Another member of the Mormon Battalion, Henry Mitchell Johnson, was born July 12, 1821, in Dearborn County, Indiana. He went with his mother to Jackson County, Missouri, in 1832, but in November of the same year, they were driven out of that county, causing him to walk bare-footed over the frozen prairie to another Mormon settlement in Missouri. In 1848 he began the trek westward from Nauvoo to Utah. During this journey he enlisted in the Mormon Battalion and marched with them to California. He arrived in Utah, October 24, 1848 and later on served as a minute man in the Indian wars there.[46]

Samuel Brown was born on October 29, 1832, in Cincinnati. He migrated to Utah in 1852, settling in Filmore, Utah. While serving a mission in the White Mountains, Samuel helped found a settlement there. While on his mission, Samuel was shot by Ute Indians, dying for the faith.[47] James Burch, one of the original settlers of Ogden, was also born in Cincinnati. In addition to being a high councilor and missionary, James served in the Utah militia during the Johnston Army troubles in 1857-1858, and took part in defending Echo Canyon. He was also a farmer and a broom-maker as well as a police officer and school trustee.[48]

The First Branches Are Established

With all these converts, it was natural that branches of the Church of Jesus Christ of Latter-day Saints be established in the Cincinnati area. Lyman Wight probably created the first Cincinnati branch in 1831. And, as was previously mentioned, sometime before 1835 Robert Culbertson organized one in Kentucky, along the Licking River. In addition to these, there were also branches in Mill Creek, Hamilton County; Mason, Warren County; Washington Court House, Fayette County; Waynesville, Warren County; Dayton, Montgomery County; and Switzerland County, Indiana. Later sources, especially early LDS newspapers, speak consistently in these early years of small but thriving branches in the Cincinnati area, "well united and in excellent spirits."[49] These were presided over by the likes of Samuel Bennett (1842),[50]

45. Jenson, *Latter-day Saint Biographical Encyclopedia*, 4:739.

46. Ibid, 4:750.

47. Ibid, 2:598.

48. Ibid, 2:242.

49. *Journal History*, November 14, 1849, 6.

50. *Times and Seasons,* 1:185.

Joshua Grant (1843),[51] John Bair (1845),[52] John W. Crippin (1845),[53] and many others.

Suffice it to say, Cincinnati lived up to its early promise as a field white already to harvest. Not only did many converts come from Cincinnati, but these converts contributed greatly, often at great sacrifice, to the rise of the LDS Church in Missouri, Illinois, Utah, and the Cincinnati area itself.

51. Smith, *History of the Church*, 5:337.

52. *Times and Seasons*, 15 March 1845, Conference Minutes, 6:841-842.

53. Ibid, 1 June 1845, Conference Minutes, Vol. 6, No. 10, p. 916.

CHAPTER 2

A Way Station to the West (1840-1890)

by Bradley J. Kramer

> Wherefore the decree hath gone forth from the Father that they shall be gathered in unto one place upon the face of this land, to prepare their hearts and be prepared in all things against the day when tribulation and desolation are sent forth upon the wicked. (D&C 29:8)

If Mormons are known for anything, it is for their large part in settling the western United States. This was no accident of history. Consistently converts were encouraged to migrate from their comfortable homes westward to the center of the Church, which changed as the Church was driven west by persecution. Kirtland, Ohio, came first, quickly followed in succession by Independence, Missouri, then Nauvoo, Illinois, and finally Salt Lake City, Utah. But throughout the nineteenth century, the counsel remained the same: gather westward, for mutual protection and economic security.[54]

Although Cincinnati was never identified as a center of the Church, few policies affected the Mormons in Cincinnati more during this time. Because of it, they were continually emigrating west during most of the nineteenth century. This kept the Mormon population in Cincinnati disproportionately small despite numerous conversions. In 1833 the entire membership of the Cincinnati Branch at that time went with the Higbees to Jackson County, Missouri. Rejoining their original missionary, they relocated on the Big Blue and Round Grove Creek with Lyman Wight.

---

54. James B. Allen and Glen M. Leonard, *The Story of the Latter-day Saints* (Salt Lake City, Utah: Deseret Book Company, 1976), 73.

As Simeon Carter wrote on December 11, 1832:

> I took Brother Stevens, and came to this place [Cincinnati], and since I came here, I have baptized four. Some others are ready and waiting. The Lord is at work here, and O, that he would do a great work, for great is the wickedness and unbelief. I have baptized in all about seventy, and the Lord has kept me and supported me. The church at this place [Cincinnati] is expecting to go up to Zion [Jackson County, Missouri] next summer.[55]

It is not known when exactly these migrations occurred. Perhaps, as with the Higbees, many people in the branch waited until there were sufficient numbers to merit a larger and somewhat safer migration. Perhaps they traveled in small groups, whenever individual members felt ready. However they occurred, these continual migrations, although supplemented with a substantial number of converts and immigrants from other areas, kept the LDS community in the Cincinnati area relatively small throughout the balance of the nineteenth century.

Nevertheless, because of the Queen City's economic and geographic importance, Cincinnati figured prominently as a regional center for the Church throughout most of the nineteenth century. It was a kind of "way station"—where church leaders and missionaries would pass through and hold regional conferences, where otherwise unacquirable supplies could be had, where immigrants could rest and gather strength for the trek west, and where information about the Church could be gathered and disseminated to the rest of the nation.

Cincinnati Hosts Regional Conferences

In the ten years since 1830, Cincinnati had nearly doubled in size from 24,831 to 46,338.[56] By 1840 a prime location on the Ohio River combined with steamboat travel and several canals connecting it to the fertile Ohio heartland had set Cincinnati firmly on a solid economic foundation for decades to come. With the addition of a large number of immigrants from Germany and Ireland, Cincinnati continued its meteoric growth and quickly became the second largest industrial center in the United States. This growth was so impressive that it caused one local booster to boast that "within one hundred years from this time [1841], Cincinnati will be the greatest city in America; and by the year of our Lord two thousand, the greatest city in the world."[57] Its growth slowed later on with the advent of the railroad, but still few would challenge Cincinnati's place as the one of the preeminent midwestern cities of the nineteenth century. It was the "hub" of its region, a natural focal point for the Church and its activities in the area, especially for regional conferences. But first the branch there had to be reorganized.

55. Journal History.

56. *U.S., Sixth Census: or, Enumeration of the Inhabitants of the United States, As Corrected at the Department of State, 1840* (Washington, D.C.: Blair and Rives, 1841), 289-344.

57. Daniel Hurley, *Cincinnati: The Queen City*, bicentennial ed. (Cincinnati, Ohio: Cincinnati Historical Society, 1988), 33.

The 1840 Reorganization

After the departure of the Higbees and other early members of the Church, the branch in Cincinnati had apparently ceased to exist. There were still members in the area, however, and according to John E. Page's September 23, 1840, letter to the Church in general, they were very devout if few in number:

> Elder Hyde and myself have been treated with respect, and had the greatest attention paid us by the brethren and sisters; and by gentlemen and ladies of the first class in society, we have been made welcome very heartily to their dwellings and comforts of life. When we separate from them they grip our hands with tears standing full in their eyes, bidding farewell, and often leave something noble with us to help us on our mission; and a firm promise that they will duly reflect on the great things which we have told them.[58]

Orson Hyde

John said he had baptized thirteen people in Cincinnati[59] and added that he had a vision from the Lord "which manifested the present state of the world respecting the Jews, Jerusalem, the remnant of Israel, and also the Gentile world. As hasty summer fruit, so is this nation; as a vineyard of grapes fully ripe, ready to be gathered for the press, so are all the nations of the earth." John then went on to request "some faithful and competent elder to this place, to nurse the seed or word that has been sown here."[60] As a result of John Page's request, Samuel Bennett was appointed to preside over the Cincinnati Branch.[61]

In fact John E. Page and Orson Hyde found that there was so much missionary work to do in Cincinnati, Dayton, Franklin, Warren County, and a place called Milton that they lingered in the area too long and had to be reproved by the First Presidency for delaying their mission to dedicate Palestine for the return of the Jews.[62] It was undoubtedly with a certain amount of sadness these missionaries left an area that had been very good to them.

The 1841 Conference

The first regional conference held in the Cincinnati area occurred at Daniel Burch's house in Springdale Township, Hamilton County, on September 4, 1841, and it drew Church leaders from all over the Cincinnati area:

> Bro. A.L. Lamoreaux represented the Mill creek Branch, consisting of about 30 members, including 1 Elder, 2 Priests and 3 Teachers, all in good standing. Bro. Josiah Clark represented the Cincinnati Branch, consisting of 41 members, including 4 Elders, 1 Priest, 1 Teacher, and 1 Deacon, all in good standing. Bro. James Culberson represented the Licking Branch, in Kentucky, consisting of 9 members, including 3 Elders, all in good standing. Bro. John Bair represented the Switzerland county Branch, Indiana, consisting of 23 members in good standing.[63]

58. Smith, *History of the Church*, 4:201.

59. Ibid, 4:202.

60. Ibid.

61. Ibid.,4:204.

62. Roberts, *A Comprehensive History of the Church*, 2:45.

It, like most of the regional conferences at this time, seemed to be a two-day combination business meeting and revival. Part of the meeting was spent reorganizing branches and ordaining elders. The other included bearing of testimonies and preaching. All meetings began with songs and prayers. During this conference, speakers addressed the rise of the Church, the principles of the gospel, the second coming of Christ, and the gathering of Israel. It is interesting to note that even then the Sunday sessions were the better attended. At the end of his article concerning the conference, Andrew L. Lamoreaux pled with the *Times and Seasons* readership for more missionaries: "The Brethren from the different Branches expressed a great want of preaching. The doors for preaching are opening daily, as the harvest is truly great; my prayer to God is that He may send forth more laborers into the vineyard."[64]

Brigham Young

The 1843 Reorganization

During the summer of 1843 the Cincinnati Branch was again reorganized by three members of the Council of the Twelve Apostles: Heber C. Kimball, Orson Pratt, and John E. Page. Heber C. Kimball and Orson Pratt continued with their missions eastward while John E. Page remained behind. As soon as his fellow apostles were gone, John E. Page nullified the reorganization and reestablished the old one. A few days later Brigham Young, Wilford Woodruff, and George A. Smith visited Cincinnati, and reprimanded John E. Page and told him it was not right for one of the Twelve to undo what three had done. The new organization was reestablished at that time.[65]

The 1844 Conferences

In contrast with the 1841 conference, the 1844 conference had a much more specific purpose. During the fall and winter of 1843-44, the Church leadership concluded after many efforts that the United States government was deaf to their claims of mistreatment especially by mobs that had driven them from their homes in Missouri and threatened to do likewise in Illinois. It was therefore decided that Joseph Smith should run for the Presidency to publicize the Church's case, and elders of the Church were sent out to present this case to the public. One of those sent was Lyman Wight. Of this experience he wrote to Joseph Smith:

> On the 26th [of May, 1844] we reached Cincinnati, at 6 o'clock p.m. Elders [Brigham]Young and [Heber C.] Kimball went to visit the Church in that city, whilst I changed our luggage on board the boat Neptune for Pittsburgh. All the passengers on board the Louis Phillippe being bound for Pittsburgh came with us.
>
> At 8 a.m. on the 27th, we held a conference with the Elders in Cincinnati. I addressed them on the subject of politics, and observance of duty, and the great need of reformed government. I was followed by Brothers Kimball and Young on the same subjects.

63. A.L. Lamoreaux, "Conference Minutes," *Times and Seasons,* 1 November 1841, 3:590.
64. Ibid.
65. Jenson, *Latter-day Saint Biographical Encyclopedia*, 1:92.

Lorenzo Snow

William Watkins

We then instructed them to have 2,000 copies of your views on the Power and Policy of the Government printed, and for the elders to scatter them with the velocity of lightning and the voice of thunder.[66]

A month after that conference in Cincinnati, Joseph Smith and his brother Hyrum were murdered by a mob at the small jail in Carthage, Illinois. Amasa Lyman and Lorenzo Snow, two members of the Council of the Twelve, were in Cincinnati when they heard of Joseph's death. In his autobiography Lorenzo Snow wrote:

> When this terrible news reached me, I was near Cincinnati, to which place I immediately repaired, and found the Apostle, Amasa Lyman, who had just arrived from Nauvoo with intelligence of the martyrdom, and with counsel and instructions to the Saints and elders. The news of this sad event, of course, came wholly unexpected, and struck me with profound astonishment and grief, which no language can portray.[67]

William Watkins, a Seventy assigned to Kentucky, was near Georgetown, Kentucky, at the time when he suddenly "became perfectly dark in my mind and quite discouraged":

> I sought to overcome this feeling by calling on the Lord for help, but could not continue. As it were, a voice made an impression on my mind to go to Cincinnati. A boat had just come up the river and docked. I stepped on board and the first person I met was Elder George J. Adams. Being very well acquainted with him I told him freely of my feelings. He said, "Brother William, I have sorrowful news. Our Prophet and our Patriarch were murdered in Carthage Jail and I am now on a mission to notify the elders to return home immediately." The same day I got on a boat and went to St. Louis and from there took boat to Nauvoo. It was a serious and trying time. Few of the elders had yet arrived and the condition of the Saints was mournful in the extreme. Our enemies were rejoicing in what had been done, yet full of fear. History, of course, gives a full account of these perilous times.[68]

It is also interesting to note that a year earlier Wilford Woodruff, then in Cincinnati, had a dream portending this tragic event:

> On the night of their arrival in Cincinnati, Elder Woodruff dreamed that Joseph would again be arrested and tried in Illinois, and the same night Brigham Young dreamed that the Twelve were called home.[69]

After the death of Joseph Smith, another special conference was held December 8, 1844. Joseph Smith's death caused a leadership crisis in the Church with some vying for leadership. Most members of the Church understood that when the President of the Church died the priesthood keys of that office passed to the Quorum of the Twelve Apostles. These people therefore

66. Smith, *History of the Church,* 7:137.

67. Eliza R. Snow, *Biography and Family Record of Lorenzo Snow* (Salt Lake City, Utah: Deseret News Company, 1884), 79-80. Grammar has been standardized.

68. *Autobiography of William Lampard Watkins,* typescript, Brigham Young University Special Collections, Provo, Utah, 2.

69. Matthias F. Cowley. *Wilford Woodruff: Fourth President of The Church of Jesus Christ of Latter-day Saints—History of His Life and Labors As Recorded in His Daily Journals* (Salt Lake City, Utah: Deseret News, 1909), 189.

followed Brigham Young, as President of the Quorum of the Twelve Apostles. However, some members saw value in Sidney Rigdon's attempt to set himself up as a guardian of the Church. Sidney Rigdon was subsequently excommunicated for his unwillingness to follow Brigham Young and the Twelve and for drawing others after him. The purpose of the conference in Cincinnati was therefore to "ascertain how the saints stood in regard to the expulsion of Elder Rigdon, as some of the members of the branch had manifested a disposition in favor of Elder Rigdon as president of the church, in opposition to the Twelve, thereby causing contention and disunion in the branch."

John W. Crippin spoke on "the necessity of union in order to carry forth the work of the Lord in this part of his vineyard. He went on to show the bad effects of disunion and the good effects of union by referring to sacred and profane history."[70] John W. Crippin went on to state that "that those who were in favor of the present organization under the Twelve, could not fellowship those who opposed them. And also that it was necessary that the minds of the saints should be had, in order to produce a union, establish order, and stop controversy in our prayer meetings."

> The President then called on each member present to state his mind concerning this matter, and they were all in favor of the Twelve being the leaders of this last kingdom, until the great God in his infinite wisdom shall see fit to do otherwise.

The conference then resolved that "we will not permit any one to preach in this branch, who is not decidedly and unequivocatingly in favor of the present organization, under the Twelve."[71]

In addition to these conferences, another was held in New Trenton, Franklin County, Indiana, on November 6 and 7, 1844. David Pettegrew, who had once lived in the area, presided. Of this conference it was written that "a good feeling prevailed, the Spirit of God was made manifest. President David Pettegrew baptized nine persons, and many were believing."[72]

The 1845 Conferences

A regional conference was again held on March 8, 1845, in Waynesville, Ohio. It was attended by representatives of the Clinton, Indiana Branch; the Washington, Fayette County Branch; the Waynesville, Warren County Branch, the Clinton County Pleasant Grove Branch, Indiana; the Dayton Branch, the Green County Sugar Creek Branch, Indiana, and the Cincinnati Branch. This conference again addressed unity and loyalty to the Twelve under Brigham Young. It resolved to "support the Twelve as the Presidency of the church, according to revelation." It also resolved that elders and members should observe the Word of Wisdom or the Mormon health code.[73]

70. J. W. Crippin, Conference Minutes, *Times and Seasons*, 15 January 1845, 6:781.

71. Ibid.

72. Smith, *History of the Church,* 3:315.

73. Ibid, 6:842.

These measures seemed to work. On June 1, 1845, the Cincinnati Branch held another conference, this time at the home of Elder Pugh. During this conference it was reported that "there is more union existing in this branch than there had been for the last three years, for which we give God the glory."[74]

In 1849, *The Frontier Guardian,* a church-owned newspaper printed in Kanesville, Iowa, referred to the Church in Cincinnati:

> The Branch in that place seemed to be well united and in excellent spirits. We have received the minutes of their conference, and are pleased with their promptness and decision."[75]

In December 1849, Eli B. Kelsey visited the Cincinnati Branch as he traveled from Council Bluffs, Iowa, to Great Britain on his second mission. On December 5, he visited the home of Elder Frederick Merryweather on Vine Street between Fourth and Fifth. There he was reunited with Elder George P. Dykes, who was to travel with him to England and who had left Council Bluffs with him. However, he had gone ahead when Elder Kelsey had visited his wife's relations in Madison, Indiana. Elder Kelsey preached to a small but attentive congregation of Saints and reported that the branch was presided over by an Elder Miles and consisted of about seventy members in "moderate standing."

Elder Kelsey slept at the home of Brother Richard Pettit, and Elder Dykes slept at the home of Brother Merryweather. Brother Merryweather provided them with some medication and other necessary items and Sister Pettit washed their clothing and prepared it for the voyage. The Saints collected money for these Elders. On the morning of December 7, they boarded the steamboat Hibernie for Pittsburgh.[76]

Local Firms Supply Printing Materials

Given its prominence and the fact that it was "just up the river," Cincinnati undoubtedly furnished the Church with many essential goods and services for the building up of their settlements in Missouri and Illinois. One important contribution was with printing supplies, including presses, plates, and even paper. *The Evening and Morning Star,* the *Book of Commandments, Times and Seasons,*[77] Emma Smith's hymnal,[78] and even the third edition of the Book of Mormon were printed on paper acquired in Cincinnati.

74. Ibid, 6:916.

75. *Journal History,* 14 November 1849, 6.

76. Eli B. Kelsey, Journal, Church Archives, Historical Department, Church of Jesus Christ of Latter-day Saints, Salt Lake City, Utah.

77. "Apology,*" Times and Seasons,* March 1840, 1:74.

78. "HYMNS!! HYMNS!!*," Times and Seasons,* 1 November 1840, 2:204.

Printing Presses

W.W. Phelps

In September 1831, W.W. Phelps, a New York newspaperman who had only joined the Church three months before, was assigned to go to Cincinnati and buy a press and type in order to publish church-related material in Missouri. This he did, setting up a print shop in Independence, Missouri. There he published thirteen editions of the *The Evening and Morning Star* and began work on the *Book of Commandments*, a precursor to the *Doctrine and Covenants* containing Joseph Smith's early revelations. For over a year this little press was in operation, until it was destroyed by a mob on July 20, 1833.[79] A number of copies of the *Book of Commandments* were, however, salvaged.

In 1848 the Church again turned to Cincinnati for a press and printing supplies. This time Orson Hyde, on his way back from Washington, stopped in Cincinnati to buy "type, fixtures, and a printing press" from the Cincinnati Type Foundry. By 1849 he and John Gooch had set up shop in Kanesville, Iowa, and were producing the *Frontier Guardian*, a semimonthly newspaper, which for nearly a year and a half was the only LDS periodical published in the United States.[80]

Plates for the Book of Mormon

Another important contribution Cincinnati made to the Church involved printing of the third and fourth editions of the Book of Mormon. By 1840 there was much talk about another edition of the Book of Mormon. Despite the extreme persecution the Church had undergone in Missouri, demand had quickly outstripped supply and additional copies were badly needed. There were also a number of printer's errors in the first edition that required correcting. Nevertheless because of the persecution, no money was available for the project. All available resources were required to relocate to Illinois the many members of the Church who had been driven from their homes with little more than those things they could carry. For the time being, the matter seemed settled.

One spring day in 1840, however, Ebenezer Robinson, one of the printers of *Times and Seasons* along with Don Carlos Smith, was walking to his Nauvoo office when he received a spiritual manifestation:

> It seemed that a ball of fire came down from above and striking the top of my head passed down into my heart, and told me, in plain distinct language, what course to pursue and I could get the Book of Mormon stereotyped and printed.

After the manifestation, Ebenezer managed to get permission to print four thousand copies but little else. The money was simply not available. "Brother Robinson," Joseph Smith told him, "if you and Carlos get the Book of Mormon stereotyped you will have to furnish the money."

79. Peter Crawley, "A Bibliography of the Church of Jesus Christ of Latter-day Saints in New York, Ohio, and Missouri" *BYU Studies*, 12 (Summer 1972): 465.

80. Peter Crawley, "The Constitution of the State of Deseret" *BYU Studies*, 29 (Fall 1989): 16.

The two printers tried zealously to raise the required money but after much effort only managed to acquire $145. With such a small amount, Don Carlos gave up on the prospect of a new edition and asked Ebenezer to use the money to go to Cincinnati and purchase paper for the press. Ebenezer agreed, partially:

> I said, "Yes, I will go, but I will not come home until the Book of Mormon is stereotyped," for it was as fire shut up in my bones, both day and night, that if I could only get to Cincinnati the work could be accomplished. [Don Carlos] replied that "that was out of the question, as it could not be done with our limited means." Brother Hyrum Smith also said it could not be done, but Brother Joseph Smith did not say it could not be done, when I told him, but he said, "God bless you."[81]

Upon arriving in Cincinnati, Ebenezer quickly bought some paper and had it loaded aboard a riverboat for shipment to Nauvoo. With only $105.06¼ to his name, Ebenezer next experienced what he called a trial of his faith:

> The adversary of all righteousness said to me, "Get more paper and some type and go home; it is folly to think of getting the Book of Mormon stereotyped, for you can not do it." I replied that "I came for that purpose, and did not propose to return until it was done." but I assure you he made the big drops of sweat roll from my face, but I did not give up to him for one instant, or swerve from my purpose, although I was there a stranger in a strange city, not knowing a single person there, except those who came with me on the steamer.

Firm in his resolve Ebenezer put a copy of the Book of Mormon in his pocket and went looking for a stereotype foundry. He found one on Pearl Street but his reception there was not as he had expected:

> [A]s I stepped into the office a feeling of horror came over me and it seemed as though I was in prison. A gentlemanly-appearing man was there, and I asked him what they charged for stereotyping a book, giving him the size as near as I could without naming or showing him the book. He told me what they charged for one thousand ems, a term which I understood. I then asked him if there was another stereotype foundry in the city. He said, "Yes, one in Bank Alley, off Third Street, owned by Gleason and Shepherd." I felt in an instant that that was the place for me to apply to, and bidding the gentleman "Good day," breathing freer when I stepped into the street.

Ebenezer quickly found the establishment of Gleason and Shepherd, which was later renamed Stearns and Shepherd, and asked for the proprietors:

> A gentleman stepped forward and said, "My name is Gleason." I said, "I have come to get the Book of Mormon stereotyped." Mr. Shepherd stepped forward and said, "When that book is stereotyped I am the man to stereotype it." I then handed him the book and told him what size type I wanted it done in. He took the book and went to a case of type the size I

---

81. Ebenezer Robinson, *The Return* 2 (May 1890): 259.

had named, and set up one line and counted the ems in the line, then counted the number of lines in the page and multiplied the two numbers together, and then counted the number of pages in the book, and multiplied the number of pages by the number of ems in a page, when he said the stereotyping would amount to five hundred and fifty dollars. I told him that I had one hundred dollars to pay in hand, and would pay two hundred and fifty dollars more in three months, or while he was doing the work, and the remaining two hundred dollars within three months after the work was done. He said he would do that, and sat down and immediately wrote out a contract accordingly, which we both signed.

After the contract was signed, Ebenezer told Mr. Shepherd that he needed to see a bookbinder. Instead of just pointing the way or giving directions, Mr. Shepherd took Ebenezer by the arm and walked him there:

> [W]e went directly to the bookbinder, who said he would bind two thousand copies in good leather for two hundred and fifty dollars; which was twelve and a half cents apiece. I told him I would give him eighty dollars while he would be doing the work, and the remainder within six weeks after the work was done. He agreed to that, and wrote out a contract to that effect, which we both signed.

Ebenezer next needed more paper and Mr. Shepherd again escorted him to a paper warehouse. When they discovered that the owner was not present, Mr. Shepherd suggested that they all meet at his foundry the following morning. This they did, but the transaction was not without a complication:

> After we had concluded our bargain the paper dealer said, "Mr. Robinson, you are a stranger here, and it is customary to have city reference in such cases when we deal with strangers." Mr. Shepherd stepped forward and said, "I am Mr. Robinson's backer, sir." "All right," said the paper dealer, "you can have the paper, Mr. Robinson."

In short Mr. Shepherd guided Ebenezer nearly every step of the way, leading him to the right people, advising him, even vouching for him when he hardly knew the man. All in all his behavior was mystifying until he explained it to Ebenezer a full year later. As Ebenezer wrote:

> In June, 1841, I went to Cincinnati and settled all up with Mr. Shepherd, and paid him what was due him (his bills altogether amounting to about $1,000,), when he arose and said, "Mr. Robinson, do you want to know what made me do as I did when you came here last summer, it was no business way, it was not what I saw in you, but what I felt here," putting his hand upon his heart

But Mr. Shepherd was only part of the miracle Ebenezer enjoyed. The providing of the financial means to print the Book of Mormon was another:

> [T]here I was, a stranger in a strange city, with contracts on hand amounting to over one thousand dollars on which only one hundred had been paid, and board bill due and nothing to pay with. I confess that for a time, viewed from a worldly standpoint, it looked quite gloomy, but I never for a moment lost faith in the final success, or literal fulfillment of the previous promise of the Lord made to me in Nauvoo. In the meantime I had written to Brother Don Carlos Smith telling him what I had done, and

also to several brethren in the eastern states requesting them to get subscribers for the book, offering them one hundred and twenty books for every one hundred dollars sent us in advance, in time to meet our engagements. It was several weeks before I received a response.

The first money I received, Brother Don Carlos Smith sent me a twenty dollar bill on the state bank of Indiana, . . .This relieved me of present financial embarrassment. Not long after this, my brother, Joseph L. Robinson, who resided in Boonsville, Oneida County, New York, whom I had baptized into the Church, when on a mission to that state in the summer and fall of 1836, sent me a draft on the Leather Manufacturer's Bank of New York City, for $96. . . . Brother John A Forgeus, of Chester County, Pennsylvania, who now resides at Little Sioux, Harrison County, Iowa, then a perfect stranger to me, whom I had never seen, sent me a draft on a Philadelphia bank for two hundred dollars, as a loan, which I afterwards paid him in Nauvoo. Several other brethren sent me money in advance for books, so that I paid Mr. Shepherd all his money before it became due, and gave the bookbinder eighty dollars on his contract before he had done any work on it. . . .All in all Ebenezer was quite successful. In his own words, he later wrote:

I had the printing progressing before the stereotyping was finished, so that by the time the last twenty-four pages of stereotype plates were finished, the printer had the book all printed, except the last form, of twenty-four pages, and the printed sheets were in the hands of the bookbinder being folded, so that soon after this last form was printed, the bookbinder had several hundred copies bound, ready for me to deliver to those who had advanced their money for the books. This was strictly in accordance with the instruction I received in the first manifestation made to me in Nauvoo.

Thus the work was accomplished, and all paid for before the time specified in the contracts, and I had nearly one thousand copies left. The work was finished in October.

I then purchased from Mr. Shepherd and other parties several fonts of type, and material for a stereotype foundry and bookbindery, and winter's supply of news and book paper, and took to Nauvoo, a considerable portion of which I paid for down, and got credit for the balance. Mr. Shepherd endorsed one note for me of four hundred dollars, payable in four months, which I sent him before it became due.[82]

This impression was confirmed by others. Later on in 1840 John E. Page wrote the following to the First Presidency:

I must save a place in this communication to make some remarks concerning Brother Ebenezer Robinson. I can say, in truth and soberness, that he merits the esteem and confidence of the Saints and all good men for his diligence and economy while getting the Book of Mormon stereotyped, &c., here. The honest and frank course he has pursued towards the gentlemen with whom he has been concerned in business (viz., Messrs. Shepherd, Stearns, and others), has won their everlasting respect and esteem, judging from their own manifestations to me.[83]

---

82. Ibid, 260-62.

A third edition of the Book of Mormon of 2,000 copies was printed by Don Carlos Smith and Ebenezer Robinson in Nauvoo, in 1840, from these plates made in Cincinnati. A fourth edition was also printed from these plates in Nauvoo in 1842.

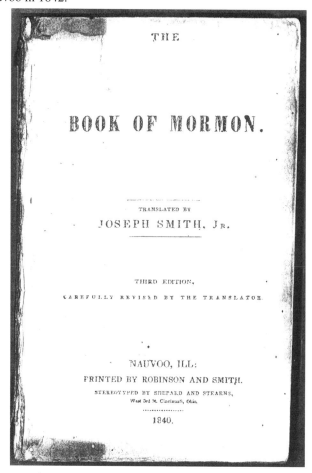

Title Page from the 1840 Edition of the Book of Mormon

83. Smith, *History of the Church,* 4:201.

Cincinnati Printers Publish Church Books

Not only did the city of Cincinnati furnish the material for the Church to publish its books and periodicals in other places, a number of books were published in town as well. This is hardly surprising. By 1830s Cincinnati had become the fourth largest publisher of books in the United States—behind New York, Philadelphia, and Boston. By the end of the decade, Cincinnati published between one and two million books, among them the staple McGuffey readers.[84] The publishing industry in Cincinnati was also know for its "state of the art" equipment. Its publishing houses quickly took advantage of steam paper-milling, stereotyping, and power presses. Given this situation, it was only logical for the Church to seek to publish books in Cincinnati, especially when it wanted to reach a large number of readers. Two books on the Missouri persecutions, *Facts Relative to the Expulsion of the Mormons or Latter-day Saints, from the State of Missouri, Under the "Exterminating Order"* and *An Appeal to the American People,* are good examples

A Defense of the Church

In May 1839, after the Church had been violently driven from their lands in Missouri by mobs, a general conference was held in Quincy, Illinois, in part to see what could be done about this injustice. As part of this effort John P. Greene, a brother-in-law of Brigham Young and a long-time leader of the Church, was appointed to represent the Church's position to the people of Cincinnati, Pittsburgh, Philadelphia, and New York and attempt to get their support. John took with him a considerable number of "letters, minutes, public statements, and sworn affadavits [sic], composed by Latter-day Saints and non-Mormons alike, which give evidence for the injustice the Mormons suffered in Missouri."[85]

John took these documents and used them to present the Church's case to the Democratic Committee of Cincinnati in the chapel of the Cincinnati College, which later became the University of Cincinnati, on June 17, 1839. The committee was moved by John Greene's presentation and made the following resolutions:

> Resolved, That we have heard with sensations of the deepest regret the tale of wrong and suffering, inflicted on the people called Mormons, while resident citizens of Missouri, by an armed mob of the people of that State, who, it appears to us, acted under the advice and orders of Governor Boggs, and whose conduct we believe to be an outrage upon every principle of justice, and all law, human and divine; alike disgraceful to the actors, and to the State which neglects to bring them to punishment.
>
> Resolved, That we will cheerfully aid, by our means, the widows and

---

84. Walter Sutton, *The Western Book Trade: Cincinnati as a Nineteenth-Century Publishing and Book-trade Center* (Columbus, Ohio: Ohio State University Press, 1961), 67-68.

85. Clark V. Johnson, ed., *Mormon Redress Petitions: Documents of the 1833–1838 Missouri Conflict* (Salt Lake City, Utah: Bookcraft, Inc., 1992), 3.

fatherless, made so by the hand of ruthless violence, in this most unprin-
cipled and disgraceful transaction, and we assure the surviving sufferers
of our sincere sympathy in their distress, and will extend to them as far as
in our power, that support which they so much need to alleviate their
present wants, and to restore them to their just rights.

Resolved, That the story of wrongs done the Mormon people, which we
have just heard, almost surpasses human credulity; and we believe they
ought to be spread before the American people and the world, in the best
authentic form that can be obtained.

Resolved, That a committee of four persons (of whom the chairman of
this meeting shall be one) be appointed to collect all the facts in their
power, and present them to a future meeting in the form of a preamble
and resolutions.

Resolved, That all those who may think proper to contribute, may do so
by handing over the same to the chairman of this meeting, who will keep
a list of names, and the amount donated by each, and report the same to
the next meeting.

Resolved, That the proceedings of this meeting be published in the City
newspapers.[86]

This committee apparently then followed up their firm words with
strong actions. With their influence John Greene soon published the documents he had used in his presentation. In late July or early August of 1839,
he published *Facts Relative to the Expulsion of the Mormons or Latter-day
Saints, from the State of Missouri, Under the "Exterminating Order."* This
book, printed by R.P. Brooks, had a circulation of 3,000 or 5,000 and is still
one of the main primary sources of information concerning the Mormon
problems in Missouri.

It contained Joseph Young's account of the Haun's Mill massacre, Governor Boggs's extermination order, General Clark's November 6, 1838,
speech, the "petitions of Caleb Baldwin, Lyman Wight, Joseph Smith, Alex-
ander McRae, and Hyrum Smith to Judge Tompkins" as well as a summary
of the Mormon experience in Missouri, which was signed by Edward Partridge, Heber C. Kimball, John Taylor, Theodore Turley, Isaac Morley,
George W. Harris, John Murdock, and John M. Burk.

A History of the Church

In 1840 Orson Hyde attempted a similar project also in Cincinnati. On
his way to dedicate Palestine for the return of the Jews, Orson Hyde met up
with George W. Robinson, who had a history of the Church written by Sidney Rigdon. This history had been approved at an earlier conference and was
expected to be a great aid to missionary work. Orson immediately joined in
with George thinking it especially helpful "to throw out before the world a
history of the various persecutions which this church has suffered since its
organization in 1830."[87]

86. Ibid, 55-56.

87. Orson Hyde, "Communications," *Times and Seasons* 1 (March 1840): 72.

George Robinson went immediately on to Cincinnati to procure a publisher while Orson Hyde called upon various members of the church for donations for "this very necessary work." Orson was disappointed with "some of the rich men who professed to be brethern [sic] in the church" and amazed at the generosity and faith of "some of the poor brethren" who were willing "to divide the last shilling and the last loaf" for this cause.[88] Nevertheless Orson did acquire the necessary money and on January 6, 1841 started for Cincinnati. His plan was to take the books and distribute them as his made his way east. However, the books were not ready in time and Orson opted to move on to Philadelphia. These books were collected and distributed by George Robinson for use by the missionaries under the title *An Appeal to the American People* by Sidney Rigdon. Apparently many of the books did eventually catch up with Orson Hyde for his use.[89]

Local Newspapers Print Articles on the Church

These efforts to educate the citizens of Cincinnati concerning the history and situation of the Church seem to have been very effective. Several articles in local papers were quite sympathetic.

Against the Persecution in Missouri

The following is an extract from a rather lively article published in Cincinnati's *Western Messenger*, reprinted in the December 1840 edition of *Times and Seasons*. It begins:

> Reader! Let not the word (Mormon) repel you! Think not that you have no interest in the cruelties perpetrated on this poor people! Read, we pray you, the history of this persecuted community; examine the detailed facts of these atrocities; reflect upon the hallowed principles and usages trampled under foot by ruffians; bring before your mind the violations of all law human and divine, of all right, natural and civil, of all ties of society and humanity, of all duties of justice, honor, honesty, and mercy, committed by so called freemen and Christians and then speak out, speak out for prostrate law, for liberty disgraced, for outraged man, for heaven insulted . . . It seems like some horrid dream, that these enormities, which Nicholas would have shrunk from inflicting on the Poles, have been deliberately committed in an age of peace, in a land of laws and freedom, upon our own brethren. Is it actually true, that citizens, peaceable, industrious, temperate, orderly citizens, have been driven from their property, their houses burned, the furniture broken and scattered, their crops laid waste, their stores plundered, their cattle killed, their horses stolen, their clothes stripped from them, and themselves expelled under threats of instant death? Is it true that men have been tarred and feathered, whipped till they were raw from head to foot, till their bowels gushed out, that their skulls have been knocked in, and brains scattered with musket-buts, that they have been shot down while crying for quarter, shot down unarmed and

---

88. Ibid.
89. James Sloan, clerk, "Conference Minutes," *Times and Seasons,* 3 (April 15, 1842): 761.

defenceless like hogs in a pen? Is it true that sick women have been
driven from burning houses at midnight on the snowy prairies, where they
have given birth to children on the (frozen) ground, that they have forded
rivers with helpless infants in their arms, fleeing from heartless pursuers,
that they have been insulted when their natural protectors were hid from
the murderers, that they have been violated by the guards appointed for
their defence? And were the guilty instigators and executioners of these
massacres, arsons and rapes, really men of standing, ministers of the gospel, judges, senators, military officers, and the Governor of the state?
Were not the evidence on which the narrative of each one of these cruel-
ties rests (incontrovertible), no one could conceive that such fiend-like
acts had actually been wrought by beings in human shape. Would, that,
for the honor of our nature, they could be discredited. Our statement is
strictly, (unexaggeratedly) true. It is only TOO MEAGER, TOO FEE-
BLE.[90]

The article then gives Joseph Young's graphic account of the Haun's
Mill Massacre, which, it is careful to include was "given under oath" and follows it with other accounts of tragedy, never excusing the Missouri officials:

[Mormon] Men from the country were not allowed to go to their families,
though in a suffering condition for food and firewood, the weather being
very cold and stormy. (It will be recollected that at this time there was a
most unprecedented fall of snow and severity of weather.) Much property
was destroyed by the troops in town, such as burning house logs, rails,
corn cribs, boards, &c., the using of corn and hay, the plundering of
houses, the killing cattle, sheep and hogs, and also the taking of horses
not their own, and all this without regard to owners, or asking leave of
any one. In the mean time men were abused, women insulted and abused
by the troops, and all this while we were kept prisoners.[91]

The article then goes on to condemn Missouri's treatment of the Mormons:

Now let every one on reading this tale of horror, speak out fully, fear-
lessly. Had the Mormons been pirates, blood stained, had they been Indians, girdled with scalps, they would have deserved better treatment. Let
the unsupported accusations brought against them be true, and yet the
conduct of their plunderers and murderers was utterly without a palliation
or excuse. Before the face of heaven, and in the sight of men, such acts
are devilish.[92]

The article ends with some speculation as to what caused this tragedy in
Missouri and feels that the Mormons for their part were "deluded, obstinate,
zealous, exclusive in their faith" using "vague, prophetic denunciations of an
enthusiastic sect."

90. "Outrages of Missouri Mobs on Mormons," *Times and Seasons,* 2 (1 December 1840): 235-36.
91. Ibid, 2:237.
92. Ibid.

It also, mirroring the opinion of the time, is suspicious of "the sincerity of their leading men" but on the whole lays the blame at the doors of the Missourians:

> Blind prejudice multiplied evil suspicions, enmity misconstrued natural acts, slander swelled trifles into monstrous wrongs, idle curiosity, greedy of alarm, and eager to gossip, circulated rumors. Now add that [the Mormons] were a large and growing community, allied together both by necessity and choice, and (withal prosperous), and we have an explanation of the fear, jealousy, envy and hatred felt against them (an explanation, but no justification). The same elements were active and fierce in these Missouri outrages, which have kindled the faggot, and bared the sword, and opened the dungeon in all times. These elements were bigotry, ignorance, panic. And when we talk of living in an age of enlightenment liberty, and law, let us recollect with shame the burning of the convent at Charlestown, the absurd humbug of Maria Monk, and the countless wrongs which other mobs, for as slight pretexts, have wrought in almost every State in the Union. The blaze of these other disgraceful proceedings, is lost, however, in the hot glare of this infernal outbreak.[93]

In Favor of Mormon Preaching

The following also comes from *Times and Seasons* (Thursday, December 1, 1842], reprinted from *The Daily Sun*, which was published in Cincinnati:

> On Sunday evening last, Mr. Adams, a Mormon Elder, delivered a lecture at College Hall, to a crowded house. He proved that the Book of Mormon was a record of the lost ten tribes of Israel, and that it was spoken of by the prophet Isaiah, and that its appearance would be just before the rebuilding of Jerusalem, and in an age when creeds of all kinds deluged the earth, and when the priests had turned the gospel into a trap to make money by entirely subverting the order and spirit of the gospel, which is spoken of by the prophets as a deep sleep, from which they are to be awakened by the new Book, the Book of Mormon, which will again renew the spirit of the gospel as preached by the disciples, introducing again the working of miracles, speaking in unknown tongues, revelations from God, and other wonderful knowledge and power supposed to have been taken from the earth for the last eighteen hundred years! He ridiculed with great severity, the creeds of the prevailing denominations of the day, intimated that their upholders were afraid to meet him in debate, claimed the utmost sanctity and holiness for the "Latter Day Saints," prayed for his congregation to be instructed in the ways of truth, gave newspaper editors and their reporters a slap in the mouth, and said that the self-constituted church authorities would not give up their holds of making money and a good living for the glorious truths of Mormonism without a struggle, pointed to the persecution of his people, and rejoiced exceedingly in the hope he entertained that the world would speedily be regenerated and the glorious truths of the gospel as preached by the Mormons spread to the remotest bounds of the earth.

> Whatever this new doctrine may be, it is extremely pleasing to the world, and death to the constituted church creeds of every name but that of Mor-

93. Ibid., 2:238.

mon. It is destined to spread, for every man that takes it upon him to speak in its favor, is fully competent to make out his case. One is very much surprised to see with what facility they prove their doctrine from the holy scriptures. Mr. Adams remarked, that he did not care whether a man believed the Book of Mormon or not, so that he came forward with a broken heart, believing on the Lord Jesus Christ and in baptism for the remission of sins—let him come forth, and if God did not reveal to him the truths of the Book of Mormon, he need not believe it. Mr. Adams is expected to lecture in this city again on Sunday next.

There are a few editorial remarks in the above that are worthy of our notice. Mr. Curtis states that "whatever this new doctrine is it is extremely pleasing to the world and death to the constituted church creeds of every name but that of Mormon." We think if Mr. Curtis had travelled with the Saints through their various persecutions he would not have thought the doctrine to be so extremely pleasing; his remarks however are not altogether inapplicable, for whenever truth is presented in its native simplicity to the understanding of man, it recommends itself to their consciences; it vibrates with those chords of honor and integrity that are cherished by every philanthropist and man of truth; and being of a pure and celestial nature, like the sun, it ever shines, and sheds its genial rays on all that comes within its reach; its luminous beams also "bring to light the hidden works of darkness" and hence, as Mr. Curtis has very properly said, "it is death to the constituted church creeds of every name but that of Mormon." He thinks that "it is destined to spread; for every one that takes upon him to speak in its favor is fully competent to make out his case." But what is the reason? Is it because they are men of greater erudition, talent, learning, or experience, than other men? No! They are about the same kind of beings as the rest of mankind; why then are they so competent to make out their case? Mr. Curtis says, "one is very much surprised to see with what facility they prove their doctrines from the holy scriptures." This then is the secret; their being able to prove their doctrines from the Holy Scriptures, is the reason why they are "fully competent to make out their case" this is the reason why Mormonism "is destined to spread" and this is the reason why it is "death to the constituted church creeds of every name." The bible is presented in its native simplicity, and they either die a natural death, or are killed by the Mormons with the bible.[94]

About Brigham Young

In 1872, the *Cincinnati Commercial* published an account of their correspondent's interview with President Brigham Young:

We waited over an hour for "The President," as he is called, but as there was plenty to see and plenty of people to talk to, the hour passed pleasantly. A door leading to the inner sanctum, and the King of the Mormons, the ruler of Utah, the venerable Brigham Young, stood before us.

He is a stout looking old man of 71 years, his body showing large bones, and slightly bent with the weight of time, his face smooth down to the chin whiskers, his hair frosted by many winters, his forehead broad and high, his lips firm, his eyes bright, his face kind, and his voice low and

---

94. "Mormonism, *"Times and Seasons,* 4 (1 December 1842): 28-29.

gentle. Such is Brigham Young. His troubles of the last years are telling fearfully upon him, and unless his enemies relent and give him and his Church some peace, it is evident that he will be moved hence, ere long.

Being a prisoner, and these critical times, he is very cautions what he says, even to his trusted friends.

He spoke in deep feeling of unjust prejudices which were harbored against his Church, accusing the Methodists of being particularly vindictive. He affirmed that the Mormon was a liberal church, interfering with no one, and only asking to be let alone and to worship God in their own way. He said that Methodists, Episcopalians, Catholics, and all denominations were allowed to preach in the Tabernacle, and gave numerous instances where the privileges had been granted to eastern ministers, who repaid the kindness by pitching into the Mormon religion.

In appearance and address he impresses me as a kind-hearted old man, and as for the stories about his instigating murder and robbery, I simply don't believe them. No man can be a fiend without his face showing it, and I defy man to see wickedness in the lineament of Brigham Young's face.

Against Polygamy

In 1854 the Republican Party in their first national campaign nominated John C. Fremont for president on a platform that stated, among other things, that "it is both the right and the imperative duty of Congress to prohibit in the Territories those twin relics of barbarism—Polygamy and Slavery."[95] For quite some time after that, the Republican party—from presidents Grant to Hayes to Garfield—condemned polygamy and worked actively to prohibit it. In such a Republican city as Cincinnati, it only followed that there would be articles against the practice.

On November 9, 1882, the *Deseret Evening News* quoted the Cincinnati *Times-Star*:

Polygamy should be crushed out, and when it is said that the Mormons encourage and foster it, that is the worst that can be said of them. All the evidence of impartial observers goes to show that they are honest, temperate, industrious and virtuous beyond the average of communities. Stories of a different nature, in which they are portrayed as corrupt and degraded, have generally originated with disappointed office-seekers. The truth is, that shorn of polygamy, the Mormons would undoubtedly very soon be classed among the most creditable citizens of our country.[96]

95. Allen and Leonard, *The Story of the Latter-day Saints*, 297.
96. *Deseret Evening News,* 9 November 1882.

The Queen City Entertains Apostates

Apostates also found Cincinnati a good place to spread their opinions John C. Bennett, who had served as Joseph Smith's counselor in the First Presidency but was excommunicated from the Church for immorality, embarked on a speaking tour of various eastern cities. One of his stops was Cincinnati. An advertisement in the *Cincinnati Republican* appeared on 26 July 1842:

> General Bennett, the distinguished seceder from the Mormon faith, was in town on Sunday, and stopped at the Broadway Hotel. He made so many startling disclosures of the iniquities practiced by Joe Smith on the noodles congregated at Nauvoo that his life is considered in danger of the assassin's steel. He left yesterday morning on the Robert T. Lytle for the East.[97]

Also the followers of James Strang, who asserted that he was the legitimate successor to Joseph Smith, and other apostate members of the Church were in the city. One was Gladden Bishop, who had been excommunicated during Joseph Smith's time. Bishop's presence in Cincinnati is mentioned in an 1855 letter from Elder Charles H. Basset to Elder D.L. Mackintosh:

> I arrived in Cincinnati about the middle of July, and after remaining there about a week, I was appointed to labor in Springfield, Ohio. I found a few Saints in Springfield, who received me kindly, and during my stay with them, tried to make me comfortable. I succeeded in fusing new life into some and waking them up to a desire to emigrating, and I think that several of them will go to the (Salt Lake) Valley this season. I baptized four persons, who are good Saints, and are anxious to escape to the mountains as soon as may be.
>
> Gladden Bishop is among the apostates in Cincinnati, and has adopted a part of their doctrines, and they in turn have embraced part of his; thus they have amalgamated, tho' Gladden of course, reserves the perrogative [sic] of standing at the head.
>
> In my travels I have been able to get out a few hearers for the first time, and frequently they have turned out and filled the rooms we have preached in. They come expecting to hear something about Polygamy, for they think that our religion consists of nothing but plurality of wives— and that no other doctrine is recognized as Mormonism. They hear nothing said about this principle, and go away much disappointed, and seldom come a second time. They are only prompted by curiosity, and that not being gratified, they go away, saying that they have heard nothing of Mormonism—nothing but the Bible read and commented upon . . . I have been much surprised to find so many who were once connected with the Church, now standing outside and watching, as they say, the signs of the times. I find in some counties in Ohio, that nearly half of the population have once been Mormons and in one town nearly all have been members of the Church. They say nothing to outsiders, but talk among themselves

James Strang

97. Andrew C. Skinner, "John C. Bennett: For Prophet or Profit?" in *Regional Studies--Illinois*, H. Dean Garrett, ed. (Provo, Utah: Department of Church History and Doctrine, Brigham Young University, 1995), 260.

about the progress of the work, pretending to be utterly indifferent to these things; but their uneasy countenances, and the ominous shaking of their heads, whenever Mormonism is mentioned are an index to something more in their minds than they can speak. It seems to be of no use to preach to them; they know all about it now. They have passed thro' a great variety of isms, including spiritualism, and the papers and books strewed about their houses. They will keep an Elder overnight, but would not give him a quarter of a dollar towards buying a pair of shoes, if he was barefoot, neither will they go across the street to procure a place to preach.[98]

Cincinnati Becomes a Temporary Place of Gathering

In 1855 the Church emigration policy changed, making Cincinnati a temporary place of gathering. Mormons traveling from Europe to the Salt Lake Valley usually entered the United States at New Orleans. Because of the high mortality rate of these immigrants the presidency of the Church issued the following statement:

> A place of gathering has been appointed in Cincinnati, and another in St. Louis—the former under the presidency of Orson Pratt, the latter that of Elder Erastus Snow. Orson Pratt has not yet arrived, but is expected in the ensuing season. In the meantime, Elder Orson Spencer, a very learned and talented gentleman, who is well known among the Saints, will preside in Cincinnati, and give direction to the affairs of the Church in that place.

Orson Spencer had been sent on a mission to Europe in 1852 but was kicked out of Prussia and later returned to Utah in 1853. In 1854 he was called on a mission to the United States. He spent most of his time in Cincinnati, residing there until July 1855.

On February 27, 1855, Elder Isaac Allred left Liverpool, England, with four hundred Saints and arrived in Philadelphia fifty-three days later. He left two hundred Saints there and continued to Cincinnati on the steamship *Monongahela.* Three other member families remained with him for a time in Cincinnati. They probably stopped to earn additional funds to cross the plains since Cincinnati was designated a temporary gathering place where work could be found.

Shortly thereafter, Orson Spencer announced in the *Luminary* that he was no longer in Cincinnati and that Elder John Banks would take charge of the Church in Cincinnati during his absence. Little is known of the John Banks era in Cincinnati except that missionary work continued in full force then. Stephen Walker, for instance, who later became a bishop of Peoa, Utah, was baptized by President Banks in May, 1855, where he also was ordained to the offices of deacon and teacher; and later (April 3, 1859) he was ordained a priest by his father.

Orson Spencer

---

98. *St. Louis Luminary,* April 22, 1855.

Robert Ellwood

On August 27, 1856, Joel M. Berry wrote from Cincinnati to John Taylor in New York:

> On the 30th day of July, I found myself in Cincinnati. After resting a few days I proceeded to my labors. There are about 150 Saints in this place. Since I have been here I have baptized 6, and there is a good prospect for more soon. A good spirit prevails here among the Saints.[99]

Robert Ellwood, who joined the Church in England and later became a bishop in Salt Lake City, states:

> Set sail on bord the Ship Thornton on May 3, 1856 and Landed in Castle Gardens on June 14th and Located at Cincinnati Ohio Wher their was a large Branch of the Church Where wee staid five years the last two of which I was apointed to preside over the Branch until the Summer of 1861 when we left Cincinnati to go to Florence Nebraska.[100]

An Angel Moroni Comes to Cincinnati

During this general period of history, the LDS Church made a rather important contribution to Cincinnati, supplying it with one of its more visible and intriguing landmarks. Although absolute proof is hard to come by, it is highly likely that the "Angel Gabriel" that flew atop the Salem Evangelical Reform Church for nearly a hundred years was actually the Angel Moroni from the Mormon temple in Nauvoo, Illinois.

The Salem Angel

Ever since her high school days at Woodward, Marie Dickore, a noted Cincinnati historian and genealogist, had been fascinated by the angel atop the Salem Evangelical Reform Church. The oddly prone position, the delicate wings, the gilded trumpet pressed to the angel's lips, not to mention its age, filled her with awe and puzzlement as it turned in the wind. In 1926 Marie was invited to attend a musical program at the old German Church. After the program she spoke with the minister, the Reverend. E.H. Katterhenry, and asked about the mysterious angel. Reverend Katterhenry, after learning that Marie could read old German script, showed her the church's records. As she read these records, some dating back to 1856, Marie discovered that the angel had been made for the Mormon temple at Nauvoo, Illinois, and was only later purchased by the small German-speaking congregation for use on its newly constructed church.

According to Marie Dickore, members of Evangelisch-Reformierten Salems-Gemeinde built a new church on the corner of Sycamore and Orchard streets in 1867. Probably in celebration of the end of the Civil War, the congregation decided to place an angel weathervane on their steeple and set up a committee to find a suitable figure. The first figure they obtained from Philadelphia was not liked and was discarded. The committee then heard of a second-hand figure that could be secured in Illinois. The committee bought the angel and placed it on the steeple of their church where it

---

99. *The Mormon,* September 6, 1856.

100.*The Autobiography of Robert Ellwood*, Mormon biographical sketches collection (ca. 1900-1975).

remained, one of Cincinnati's most distinctive landmarks, until 1966 when lightning knocked it off the church, and it had to be replaced.

Unfortunately the records Marie Dickore read later on disappeared, probably the victim of an unknowing cleaning committee, and it is also not clear how the angel could have survived the fire that gutted the Nauvoo temple in 1848 after it was abandoned. However, Marie Dickore made careful notes and her findings were convincing enough to satisfy Alvin F. Harlow, who published them in his book *The Serene Cincinnatians,*[101] as well as Dr. Robert D. Craig, a history professor at the Church College of Hawaii, who published his findings in *Ka Malana'i Okaue*, magazine of the Church College of Hawaii in the spring of 1968.

**The Angel as It Looked after Falling
from the Salem Church in 1966**

Despite the lack of conclusive evidence, the case for the Salem angel being the Nauvoo Moroni remains strong. The American Primitive style of the angel—with its large head, small feet, and crude features—seems consistent with the period, and the general appearance of the angel is identical to the Moroni weathervane in early drawings of the Nauvoo temple. In addition when the angel was knocked down, a close inspection of it revealed 144 patched bullet holes much larger than those made by modern rifles. These bullet holes were smoothly patched on the outside but were still jagged on the inside. Since no record exists of anyone firing at the angel while it was a weathervane for the Salem church, these bullet holes seem to reinforce the claim that it came from Nauvoo where it was used as target practice by anti-Mormon mobs.

After its fall, the angel was badly damaged, and yet its sturdy construction was still evident. It was made from sheets of tin, of a somewhat heavier gauge than what is commonly used now, and soldered together. It was gilded originally and regilded in the 1930's. And although in 1966 the bare tin

101.Alvin F. Harlow, *The Serene Cincinnatians* (New York: E.P. Dutton & Co., 1950), 186-87.

showed through the gilding in many places, this could have been due to its being hurled onto the pavement. The mere fact that it weathered the storms of more than one hundred years testifies as to how well it was made.

After the angel was blown down, the Salem church replaced it with an exact replica and gave what was left of the angel to the Nauvoo Restoration, Inc. when the new angel was installed in 1968. Despite the fact that the angel that now flies over Salem United Church of Christ, the new owners of the old Over-the-Rhine church, is a replica, many Mormons still take inspiration from it and see in it a symbol of their faith's involvement in the history of Cincinnati and a sign of good things to come.

CHAPTER 3

A Permanent Branch
(1890-1935)

*By Bradley J. Kramer
and Stanley L. Fish*

There is little information about Church in Cincinnati between 1860 and 1890. It may be that records were not kept or were lost, or that additional research needs to be done. It may be that most of the faithful Saints had gone west and the branch dwindled in the face of increasing anti-Mormon and anti-polygamy sentiment. Certainly during these years of renewed trials for the Church in Utah, there were fewer missionaries to preach in Ohio.

Whatever the reason, everything changed in the 1890s. These years brought a new era to the Church in Cincinnati. The purpose of gathering had largely been accomplished. Utah was filled with Latter-day Saints and the disputes between the Church and the federal government had for the most part been weathered and resolved. Utah had also became a state and the Church no longer practiced polygamy. For these reasons, Church leaders began slowing down the tide of immigration. Church members in other areas were told to stay where they were and build up the Church in their area. As George Q. Cannon said in General Conference in 1889, members who lived outside of Utah should "remain quiet for a while; to not be anxious to break up their homes to gather to Zion."[102]

Around this time, missionary work in Cincinnati seems to have resumed in earnest and converts began staying in the area instead of moving west. Under these conditions, and with a little help from those church members who moved to Cincinnati, it was not long before a permanent branch was established in the Queen City.

102.Allen and Leonard, *The Story of the Latter-day Saints*, 421.

Missionaries Return

Unlike the early missionaries, missionaries around this time were
called to specific geographic areas organized under specially called mission
presidents. Cincinnati, for some reason, kept switching the mission it
belonged to.

Part of the Northern States Mission

During the 1890s the state of Ohio was part of the Northern States Mission, headquartered in Chicago and presided over by Louis A. Ketch. Under
his direction Elders Michael Mauss, John B. Erekson, and W.F. Mayhew
came to Cincinnati in the spring of 1897 and began preaching. Elder Mauss
reported the following to the *Deseret News*:

> Elder Erekson and I both left our home in response to a call from God to
> assist in preaching the Gospel of Christ in the Northern States. Arriving
> in Chicago, the headquarters of this mission, I was requested to go, in
> connection with Elder W.F. Mayhew from Nephi, to Cincinnati where
> there were already two sisters, members of the Church. On our arrival, we
> climbed Price Hill, which gives one a splendid view, dedicated the city
> unto the Lord, asking him to open the way before us that we might spread
> the Gospel truths to the inhabitants.
>
> We at once began distributing tracts, and soon made many warm friends
> who did everything in their power to make us comfortable. In the course
> of a month we baptized three persons. Being the only Elders in the state
> of Ohio, we were requested to meet in conference with the Elders of
> North Indiana at Logansport. We met on the 1st and 2nd of May, eighteen
> in number, and our report was so favorable that it was thought wisdom to
> open up the state of Ohio for missionary work.
>
> Accordingly David J. Davis was appointed to preside over this confer-
> ence. The following were appointed to labor in Ohio with the promise of
> more help in the near future: D.J. David, who took up quarters at East
> Liverpool; W.F. Mayhew and W.F. Butt at Cleveland; myself and J.B.
> Erekson, this city [Cincinnati].
>
> On arriving here, May 6th, we began active work in distributing the pub-
> lished word of God and holding meetings wherever an opportunity
> afforded. The leading papers aided us to a great extent by letting people
> know that there were Mormon preachers in the city.
>
> The Lord has been very kind to us and blest us in many ways. We have
> not bought a single meal since we have been here. Yet we have not gone
> hungry in the least, and have had beds to sleep in every night.
>
> We have not forgotten to mention the great kindness of the 10 Saints here
> who do our washing and help us along in many ways. We have been
> blessed recently with the presence of our president [Louis A. Ketch] who
> will make his headquarters in this city. We have also received help a few
> days ago by the arrival of Elder Edward F. Turley from Colonia Juarez
> Mexico.
>
> We must tell you that we have organized a sabbath school which is fairly

well attended, and that we hold meetings regularly. every Sunday evening. We are greatly in need of more help, as there are nearly one million people to each Elder in this state. Truly the "harvest is great and the laborers few." [103]

In November 1897, Francis M. Lyman and Mathias F. Cowley, members of the Council of the Twelve, traveled to Cincinnati. They met with President Ketch, Elder David J. Davidson, and Elder Joseph E. Cardon. They visited the home of Joseph Forbes (Forbes' father-in-law was Noah Young, who had been associated with the Church in Nauvoo), where they met with Elders Joseph E. Wilson, Jr., Riley G. Clark, Jr., John B. Erekson, Michael Mauss, A.K. Hansen, Walter F. Mayhew, Thomas Cottle, and Edward F. Turley. Elders Lyman and Cowley were pleased by the spirit of the Elders.

Headquarters of the Middle States Mission

In May 1902, the First Presidency and the Council of the Twelve formed a new mission from parts of the Southern States Mission and the Eastern States Mission. West Virginia of the Eastern States Mission was combined with Tennessee, Kentucky, Virginia, and Ohio of the Southern States Mission to form the Middle States Mission.[104]

Ben E. Rich had been president of the Southern States Mission since 1898. The new mission was created at his suggestion and he was appointed to preside over it. On May 23, 1902, the First Presidency wrote to President Rich:

> Dear Brother, The First Presidency have decided to divide the Mission [Southern States] in two. On the lines suggested in your favor of the 13th inst, the Northern will henceforth be known as the Middle States Mission and the Southern part as the Southern States Mission. The Middle States Mission will comprise the States of Tennessee, Kentucky, Virginia, West Virginia and Ohio, over which you will have charge and presidency. We have called Bro. Ephraim H. Nye, formerly president of the California Mission to preside over the Southern States Mission.
>
> We have written President McQuarrie [John G.] of the Eastern States Mission informing him of these changes, and requesting him to transfer to you at such time and place as will be mutually agreeable and convenient, the books, records, papers, etc., that pertain to the Church in West Virginia, and to make you acquainted with the Elders and Saints and with the conditions there existing as time and opportunity will best permit.
>
> We shall also be pleased to have you do the same thing with President Nye.

By that summer the move was underway. Headquarters of the Eastern Tennessee Conference were established in Chattanooga to "enable Elder Howard H. Hale to assist in moving west of the mission headquarters to Cincinnati, Ohio."[105] In December, Ezra D. Crockett was released as president

---

103.*Deseret News*, August 17, 1897.

104.*Journal History*, 1-2.

105.Historical Record 3491: 787.

of the Middle Tennessee Conference to work at the new mission headquarters in Cincinnati.[106]

The following spring, on April 25 and 26, the presidents of various conferences in the Middle States Mission met at Cincinnati. Attending were Elders Lorenzo Crosby (Virginia), Benjamin J. Trunnell (Northwest Virginia), Loren J. Robinson (Southwest Virginia), Amos W. Neeley (Kentucky), Henry B. Elder (Southern Ohio), George A. Langston (Eastern Tennessee), and George J. Fox, Jr. (Middle Tennessee). Also present were elders then laboring in Cincinnati. These included James C. Parry, W.E. Evans, S.Y. Taylor, A.N. Sorenson, O.C. Thurber, and John F. Smith as "Canvassing Elders" and Charles H. Hyde (secretary) and Edgar Perry (corresponding secretary) of the mission office.

President Rich instructed that more work should be done in the country districts in the future, and that the elders should teach the Saints the principles of the Gospel more fully, especially the law of tithing and the Word of Wisdom, and also the necessity of faith in the divinity of the Prophet Joseph Smith's mission. Authorities of the Church preferred that the elders travel without purse and scrip as much as possible and thereby prove the people.

Between March 23 and April 25, the following work had been done in the Mission:[107]

Families visited	2,568
Tracts distributed	18,152
Books sold	1,139
Books otherwise distributed	876
Books of Mormon sold	63
Meetings held	693
Baptisms	22
Children blessed	27

The *Deseret News* of May 16 noted that on Saturday evening all the visiting brethren and the local elders assembled at the mission house in Cincinnati and were entertained by President and Sister Rich in social chat and reminiscences until 10 o'clock, when refreshments were served.

According to the 1902 and 1903 volumes of the Cincinnati Directory the Middle States Mission address was 2233 Kemper Road. A masonry building now stands there, large enough to have served as a mission home. Church leaders presumably held the above-mentioned meetings in that building.

Perhaps in conjunction with the organization of this new mission, George Reynolds, the secretary for the First Presidency, sent out the following letter on November 25, 1902 asking for the names of prospective mis-

106.Historical Record A: 831-32.
107.Historical Record A: 858-59.

sionaries who spoke German. One of the cities expressly named who had a need for these missionaries was Cincinnati:

> German speaking elders are needed in Germany, Switzerland, Turkey and Samoa; also in the cities of Cincinnati and Milwaukee, in both of which the German population is very large. As there are a number of German families belonging to the Church who are residents of your Stake, I am instructed by the First Presidency to request you to forward them the names of some German speaking brethren whom you can consistently recommend as missionaries for these places. Your prompt attention will afford them pleasure.[108]

Part of the Southern States Mission

The Middle States remained a separate mission for less than two years. In 1903 Cincinnati and the rest of Ohio again became part of the Southern States Mission over which President Rich again presided. Ohio remained part of that mission until 1926 when it again became part of the Northern States Mission, to which it had belonged prior to 1899.

Ben E. Rich was one of the great missionaries of his time, excelling in proselyting, debating, and all kinds of missionary work. He authored "A Friendly Discussion," one of the basic LDS mission tracts for many years. He served as president not only of the Southern States Mission and Middle States Mission but also of the Eastern States Mission. In all, he was directly engaged in missionary work for twenty years.

After the Middle States Mission closed, missionary work in Cincinnati proceeded slowly but with notable successes, both in Cincinnati and in outlying areas. Converts near Georgetown, such as the Prickett family—William Boler Prickett, Amos Prickett and his wife Rosella Pierce, their children Luther A., Cecil H., Virgil L., and Edith—and Edith Boling, daughter of Garland and Lucinda Ralph Boling, along with members who relocated from West Virginia and other areas, were the forerunners of the Georgetown Branch, organized in the late forties. For many years, even after there was a thriving branch in Cincinnati, the Saints in these outlying areas were left largely to themselves except for occasional visits by full-time missionaries. In fact, not until 1936 did these isolated Saints have the Melchizedek Priesthood permanently in their midst. In August of that year, President Bryant S. Hinckley of the Northern States Mission gave permission for the president of the South Ohio District to ordain Amos Prickett an elder.

Missionary work proceeded at its own pace as shown by the conversion story of G.P. Chrisman and his wife. In 1906 Joseph Smith Fish and his companion traveled through southern Ohio and brought the gospel message to the Chrismans. Although the family was not baptized then, in the following years they often extended their hospitality to elders passing through. Finally, in 1936, Alvin L. Wilkinson (Elder Wilkinson later married Frecla Kraft, a member of the Cincinnati Branch) and his companion, Ernest F. Buetler, prepared the Chrismans for baptism. The baptisms were performed by a nephew

108. *Messages of the First Presidency of The Church of Jesus Christ of Latter-day Saints* [1833-1951], James R. Clark, ed., 6 vols. (Salt Lake City: Bookcraft, 1965-1975), 4:48.

of the Joseph Smith Fish who had first introduced the Chrismans to the Gospel thirty years before. About a year after their baptisms—as it happened, about a year before their death—Brother and Sister Chrisman made the difficult eighteen-hundred-mile trip to Utah to be sealed in the temple.

Charles Anderson Establishes a Branch

Despite the fact that this increased missionary emphasis in the area yielded many converts, the Cincinnati branch as a permanent entity did not really begin until Charles V. Anderson and his wife, Christine, arrived in 1913. The Andersons came from Salt Lake City to Cincinnati to establish a manufacturing plant for household articles he had invented and patented. They intended to stay for only two years but in fact remained for twenty-three years, providing the Cincinnati Branch with strength, stability, and leadership.

At the time, President Anderson knew almost nothing about Cincinnati. He selected it only because Cincinnati "was one of the largest and most prosperous business centers in the country." President Anderson did not even know what the church situation was there. "I thought it was in the Northern States Mission and wrote Chicago," President Anderson said. He was wrong, as he quickly found out. Not only did Cincinnati belong to the Southern States Mission, but the branch there had been disorganized for many years. All this was soon to change.

In his efforts to find out what mission Cincinnati belonged to, President Anderson quickly became well acquainted with the president of the Southern State Mission, Charles A. Callis. Wasting no time, President Callis almost immediately called Charles Anderson to preside over the soon-to-be reorganized branch and rebuild it. Charles, however, hesitated:

> Thinking it would interfere with my other duties, which were quite important, I asked for time to consider. realizing it would be a difficult problem requiring much thought and labor. After a few months of deliberation and prayers to God, I told President Callis I would accept the position, and that I would give God the best that was in me.[109]

On December 2, 1914, Charles Victor Anderson was set apart as the Presiding Elder of the newly formed Cincinnati Branch. He was to serve for twenty-three years, much of this time without counselors.

109. Charles V. Anderson. *Twenty-Three Years in Cincinnati* (Salt Lake City, Utah: Self-published), 2-3.

The "Gospel Shop"

Walnut Street storefront where the branch met from 1913 to 1917

True to his word, Charles immediately threw himself into his new calling. Charles rented a small storefront on 1330 Walnut Street from Fred Gloss, a local attorney and friend of the Church. President Anderson then converted the small storefront into a meeting hall, using furniture supplied by the branch members. They called it a "gospel shop" and stayed there for about four years. Notwithstanding its size, the Cincinnati Branch was important enough to be visited by Apostle Rudger Clawson in 1915.

According to President Anderson's writings, the branch had only "eight scattered members of the Church residing in the city and vicinity" when he was first called. To increase visibility as well as foster growth, the budding branch held "entertainments," bazaars, and other social events along with regular church meetings. Growth, however, was slow. President Anderson turned to street meetings and despite some initial resistance was allowed to preach regularly on the corner of Sixth and Race from 8:00 to 9:00 on Friday evenings. In addition to President Anderson, Elders E. Hunter and A.B. Isaacson spoke. Sister Anderson and Rosa Bang supplied the singing.

Perhaps because of these efforts the branch membership increased to about twenty members and necessitated a move to a larger building. In November 1917, the branch began meeting at 63 East McMicken Street where the branch membership continued to increase to about forty to fifty members. According to President Anderson, their first baptisms were performed in the Ohio River..

First Relief Society in Cincinnati, circa 1920

The First Relief Society

While the branch was in the McMicken location, the first Relief Society in Cincinnati was formed. On January 11, 1920, Christine Anderson was called as Relief Society President with Rosa Bang as first counselor, Sarah Keller as second counselor, and Bernita Heitzmann as secretary and treasurer. The society met weekly at the home of President Anderson.

In addition to Relief Society, the branch offered priesthood meetings and a weekly class for children also at the Anderson's home. However, because of its small size, the branch did not offer a regular M.I.A. (Mutual Improvement Association—a class for teenage boys and girls)

Special Meetings

Undoubtedly the talks at the Cincinnati Branch meetings were similar to those given in any other LDS congregation at the time. Topics included "the Restoration of the Gospel" (Christian F. Datwylter, December 22, 1915), "Jesus the Christ" (Joseph Carpenter, December 26, 1915), and "Organization of the Church and Fruits of Mormonism" (Alonzo B. Isaacson, January 2, 1916).

One of the most memorable meetings occurred on Sunday, December 24, 1916. On that Christmas Eve, President Anderson said there was "a large attendance at Sunday School and an excellent spirit prevailed." President J.P. Paul spoke on the life and mission of Joseph Smith and at the close of the meeting a young man named W.J. Adams came forward and requested baptism. President Anderson wrote that Brother Adams had been attending their meetings for about a year and that immediately all the elders and most of the branch members marched down to the Ohio River where President Paul promptly baptized the young man.

Rosa and Christian Bang, Sr. with Marion D. Hanks, 1942

The entire branch then walked over to a Sister Chapin's nearby home and held an 11 P.M. sacrament meeting in which Brother Adams was confirmed and ordained a Priest. President Anderson wrote that "the slumbering neighborhood was aroused by our singing the songs of Zion and testifying of God's goodness to us and His love for His children on earth. . . . it was a Christmas Eve that will never be forgotten by those present" and "could not have been celebrated in a more beautiful and impressive manner.[110]

The Bang Family

Nearly two years before the Andersons arrived, Anna Harbreck's mother quietly introduced the Restored Gospel to another Cincinnati woman of German descent named Rosa Bang. Rosa embraced the Gospel immediately. Very soon after her discussions with Sister Harbreck, Rosa left a Book of Mormon on the table so her husband could see it when he returned from selling candy to various stores. Her husband found the book interesting and it was not long after that that Elders B.O. Carlson and George Forsythe were regular guests at the Bang home. On January 22, 1912, four years after they

---

110.*Linnean*, 14:506, February 6, 1917.

were married, Rosa and Christian Bang were baptized at the Jewish Bath House on 9th and Smith Streets, the Ohio River being frozen over at the time. As Rosa stated in talk once, "We loved the teachings when we heard it. It did not take us long to join the branch."[111] Almost immediately the Bangs became the backbone of the branch, which at the time consisted of six members, all of whom had been baptized around the same time: the Bangs, "Sister Harbreck, Brother and Sister Lee, and Sister Haun."[112]

Christian Bang, Sr. in Front of His Candy Wagon, circa 1910

According to many, Rosa Bang had some sort of special connection to the Lord. In many ways, she was the spiritual strength of the family and although the Bangs went through terrible times during the Depression, she remained steadfast and full of faith. Stanley L. Fish, who later married one of Rosa's daughters, credits her with establishing the Bangs as the stalwarts they have become in the Church in Cincinnati. With ten children—Chris, Jr., Elizabeth, Henry, Judith (who married Stanley L. Fish), Rosa (who died in infancy), Paul, Louis, Evelyn (who married Merlin Fish, Stanley's brother), Victor, and Sam—she certainly did her part to dramatically increase the size of the branch. But her influence was not just in numbers. Few families served as faithfully and frequently as the Bangs, largely, many believe, because of her influence.

Rosa's husband, Christian also added strength and support to the branch. As President Anderson later wrote:

> Upon my arrival in Cincinnati in 1913, I met a young man belonging to the Church; he was married and had two fine children. His wife was and is a most exemplary woman. When I took charge of the branch this young man grew up with it, so to speak, and stood by me nobly. When the

---

111. Rosa Bang, notes from a talk, in the possession of Judy Fish.
112. Christian Bang, Sr., personal history, in the possession of Judy Fish, 5.

branch was made an independent branch I chose him for my 1st Counselor, which position he held when I left in 1936. Trustworthy, reliable and a true friend, his name is Christian Bang, Sr.; a prosperous business man, and the father of nine splendid sons and daughters.[113]

For many years, "Mom" and "Pop" Bang were the twin pillars of the Cincinnati Branch.

The Branch Flourishes

Because of the Bangs and others, the branch had by 1921 outgrown the little McMicken Street property and it was sold. Soon the branch moved to a larger storefront at 1824 Race Street. The branch spent over two hundred dollars fixing up the building and turning it into a suitable hall. After the renovations, the hall could seat one hundred people and accommodate four Sunday School classes. The branch stayed here for about two years, their membership increasing to about seventy-five members.

In 1923, the branch again needed more space and began meeting at the Odd Fellows Temple at the corner of Seventh and Elm streets. President Anderson described the place as a "fine hall on the 6th floor" but went on to explain some challenges the branch had there:

> We were not permitted to advertise ourselves as the "Church of Jesus Christ," but merely as the "Church of *Later* Day Saints." We remained in this location for six years, our reputation improving so that there was nothing we could ask that was refused and we were permitted to advertise ourselves under our true title as the "Cincinnati Branch of the Church of Jesus Christ of Latter-day Saints." Although we have since been able to secure a chapel of our own, the reputation of the Latter-day Saints in the Odd Fellows Temple on 7th and Elm streets still stands very high.

The branch met here for approximately six years.

The "Greater" Cincinnati Branch

Soon, the proximity of the Saints in Northern Kentucky to Cincinnati led to some changes in unit boundaries, according to President Anderson:

> The Saints living in the coast cities along the Ohio River, directly opposite Cincinnati, on the Kentucky side, had hitherto belonged to the Cincinnati Branch, but the transfer retained there as members of the Southern States Mission. However, it was decided that they should belong to the Cincinnati Branch, but that the tithing paid by there into the branch should be sent to the Southern States Mission. In this way the branch was "serving two masters," so to speak, and this complicated state of affairs was burdensome and unsatisfactory, both to the branch and the mission.

Branch President Anderson had fully explained the situation to Mission President John Taylor who in turn referred the matter to the Church authorities, as a change could not be made without their sanction. Apostle Stephen

Race Street storefront where the branch met from 1921 to 1923

---

113. Anderson, 45.

L. Richards was sent to Cincinnati to study the situation, and on May 7, 1926, the authorities decided those coast cities on the Kentucky side of the Ohio River should belong to the Cincinnati Branch and be included in the Northern States Mission. These cities were Dayton [Kentucky], Bellevue, Covington, Newport, Ludlow, Latonia, Woodlawn, Ft. Thomas, in fact all cities connected by the Green Street Car Line, and commonly called Greater Cincinnati. These cities were connected with Cincinnati by several large bridges, and the business center of Cincinnati could be reached from any of these cities by a 5-cent street car fare, and furthermore, the inhabitants nearly all worked in Cincinnati.

A Chapel of Their Own

In 1929 the Cincinnati Branch reached major milestone in its history—it obtained its own chapel at 216 Orchard Street. But, as President Anderson explained, this achievement was not without its struggles and complications:

> In 1929 our fondest hopes were realized, namely we got our own chapel. It came about swiftly. On the Sunday preceding March 29, 1929, the Presbyterians held their last services in one of their churches, owned by them, situated at 216 Orchard Street, Cincinnati, and the church was offered for sale. On the above date, the branch presidency took an option on the property for 30 days, $250 for the same. The sale price being $18,500.

> When the Presbyterian ministers got to know who held the option, there was an uproar. To sell the church to the Mormons would be "sacrilege they said, and much more, and everything was done to break the option. But the option held tight.

The Orchard Street Chapel

President Noah S. Pond, who then presided over the Northern States Mission, came and viewed the property, and after a thorough investigation, approved it. Leaving almost immediately for the April General Conference of the Church, he laid the matter before the First Presidency, who approved of the purchase. On June 8, 1929, after all the papers had been properly executed and examined, the purchase price of $18,500 was paid, and the property passed into the ownership of the Church of Jesus Christ of Latter-day Saints. Not being able to annul the sale, the ministers asked President Anderson if a middleman could be used in the transfer, so it would not appear on the court house records that the Presbyterian Church had made a direct transfer to the Mormon Church. Sick of their unfriendly behavior throughout, the request was granted, and Fred Closs, an attorney, was chosen as the middleman, the property being transferred to him and from him to the Church, both transactions being executed and recorded the same day.

Remodeling cost $8,143.44, transforming the chapel into one of the handsomest houses of worship in Cincinnati. This amount included a $1,500 pipe organ. The chapel had a seating capacity of about three hundred but did not have a baptismal font. Baptisms had to be performed at the Y.M.C.A. where, according to President Anderson, branch members were treated with the "greatest of courtesy, no charge being made for the service."

The day before the date set for dedication when everything was nearly ready, a lightning storm set fire to the feedwire pole outside the chapel and the insulation of the wiring in the chapel, filling the chapel with smoke. The fire department came and it was thought the electric wiring was utterly ruined. Upon examination, however, the damage to the wiring could be repaired, and by midnight everything was all right.

Apostle Orson F. Whitney dedicated the chapel on Sunday, September 16, 1929. The chapel was filled to its uttermost capacity that memorable day. The Spirit of God rested mightily upon Apostle Whitney, whose wonderful dedicatory prayer and inspiring and powerful sermon made a lasting impression upon all present. The peace, quietness, and attention was remarkable.

Orson Whitney even mentioned this dedication in General Conference:

> During the month of September, in company with Elder Noah S. Pond, the able and amiable president of the Northern States Mission, I traversed six states of the Union, namely, Iowa, Illinois, Indiana, Ohio, Michigan and Wisconsin. We held forty meetings with the missionaries, saints and investigators, and addressed in the aggregate fully fifty percent of the Latter-day Saint population of those states. We dedicated two chapels in Ohio, one at Cincinnati, the other at Dayton, and organized a branch in that town. We also organized an Elder's quorum in Chicago, the first quorum of its kind known in any of the missions of the Church, so far as I am informed. I much enjoyed my labors, and the Lord was with us in our journeyings and in our work.[114]

This building was, so far as can be determined, the first property owned by the Church in Ohio since the days of the Kirtland exodus. In honor of the Orchard Street chapel, President Anderson, penned this rhyme:

> The little church around the corner
> Of Sycamore and Orchard Street,
> Is a sacred place of worship,
> An inviting sweet retreat.
>
> There the Mormons meet each Sabbath—
> Meet with faces smiling bright—
> Thanking God that He had brought them
> Out of darkness unto light.
>
> Do not treat their doctrine lightly,
> Do not judge them from afar.
> Go and hear them, and let reason
> Be your safely guiding star.
>
> Out of heav'n a voice is calling;
> Gently calling you and me:
> Turn from sin, obey the Gospel,
> And the Truth shall make you free.
>
> The little church around the corner
> Is echoing this gentle call:

114.Elder Orson F. Whitney, *Conference Reports of The Church of Jesus Christ of Latter-day Saints,* October 1929 (Salt Lake City: The Church of Jesus Christ of Latter-day Saints, 1880, 1897-1970), 27.

Flee from sin, and follow Jesus,
For He loves us, one and all.[115]

Early Branch Activities

Like many Mormon congregations, the Cincinnati Branch had a choir. Although this must have been a challenge for such a small group, the choir was praised by the district president and called "splendid."[116]Drama was an important part of the branch's activity from the beginning. According to President Anderson, "Dramatics is a splendid educator in good manners, use of language, conversation, self-reliance, ethics, and everything that makes a person agreeable." The branch's first entertainment was performed on Washington's birthday in 1915. Several followed, including a program given by Judith A. Bearch, a noted Utah contralto, and her daughter Rhea.

POOR FATHER

A Very Laughable Comedy in Three Acts
will be given by

The Latter Day Saints Dramatic Society

DECORATION DAY, MAY 30, 1934
In Wildy Hall, Odd Fellows Temple
Corner Seventh and Elm Streets

Characters

William Thompkins—*a hard-pressed father*	CHRISTIAN BANG, JR.
Mary Thompkins—*his wife*	FREDA KRAFT
Gladys—*a daughter*	ELIZABETH BANG
Caroline—*another daughter*	HAZEL WHEELER
Bessie—*another daughter*	JUDITH BANG
Clifford Thompkins—*psychology student*	HENRY BANG
Harold Caldwell—*always in the way*	MILTON STEINMAN
Sidney Dummel—*wealthy bachelor*	JULIUS BLACKWELDER
George Washington Brown—*trifler with truth*	THOMAS LARGE
Sergeant O'Connor—*of the Police*	RAYMOND CHAPIN
Marie—*a new French maid*	EDITH KRAFT
Vivian Laramie—*an actress*	RUTH HILL

Act I. Living Room at the Thompkins Home. Morning.
Act II. The same. That Afternoon
Act III. The same. That Night.

DUET: "My Morning," sung by Edith Kraft and Hazel Wheeler
between 1st and 2nd Act.

TAP-DANCE: Between 2nd and 3rd Act, by Milton Taylor.

ACCOMPANIST: Madeline Horton.

Adults 25c — Children 15c   Curtain 8 o'clock sharp
Tax Exemption Applied For

Playbill from "Poor Father," performed in 1934

115. Anderson, 11.
116.*Liahona* 11 (31 March 1914): 671.

In 1922 the branch produced its first play, "Our Aunt from California," on a temporary stage in the back of the Odd Fellow's Hall. The room was so small that the actors had to wait outside and enter the stage from an outside window. Despite such improvisations, the play was such a success that others were preformed, including "Half-an-Hour's Rest, which was written by President Anderson and performed by the "Deacon's Society." Soon after, the branch formed a Dramatic Society, which included boys and girls who had acted in smaller entertainments. This society quickly produced such plays as "Patty Makes Things Hum," "Safety First," and "Poor Father."Once a young sister with an important part in the production was struck by a car before the scheduled performance, but in the theatrical best tradition appeared in a wheelchair. On November 15, 1935, the LDS Drama Society performed "Raising Money in Bangville," which, according to President Anderson, created much merriment and was spoken of for years to come. The last play performed by the LDS Drama Society was on May 30, 1934, at the Odd Fellow's Hall.

Of these plays, Charles Anderson later wrote:

> We shall never forget those happy days,
> When we were practicing out little plays;
> And how we were overwhelmed with praise
> By all who came to see them.
> How sweet are the memories of those times—
> They sound like sweet echoes from silver chimes,
> Like a poem written in beautiful rhymes—
> Never again shall we see them[117]

In 1927 a full branch presidency had been set apart. Charles V. Anderson continued as president. Christian Bang, Sr. became first counselor and Robert Fletcher became second counselor until he was released in 1928, when Alvin B. Gilliam succeeded him as second counselor.

Len and Mary Hope

Members of the Church and missionaries who served in Cincinnati in the 1930s remember Len and Mary Hope and their family (three sons and three daughters). At that time they were the only African-American members of the Church in the area. Fast and testimony meetings were regularly held in their home. Following the meeting, those in attendance were treated to a feast that included fried chicken, homemade ice cream, and other delicious treats. At times there were as many as thirty guests, yet the Hopes never seemed to run out of food. They urged everyone to eat more and to come as often as possible.

The Hopes were good people with abiding testimonies of the gospel. Brother Hope often told of his conversion; it went something like this:

> I was born on a small farm in Alabama. When I was a young man, I lived with my sister. I read the Bible quite a lot, and read about the Holy Ghost.

---

117. Anderson, 34.

I felt that I needed the Holy Ghost and was determined to get it. I fasted and prayed to the Lord, but it did not come. On one occasion, I went to an old house and prayed most of the night, crying for the Holy Ghost. I was about to make a covenant that I would neither eat nor drink until the Holy Ghost came, but the spirit persuaded me not to make that covenant.

One evening, when I came home from work, my sister handed me a pamphlet and said that an Elder had left it for me. I have wondered since, why she said it was for me too. Now it had been raining for several days, and to reach the house you had to walk across a plowed field with no road or path. I can almost see that Elder with his shiny shoes and nice clothes crossing that muddy field, just to bring me a pamphlet.

As I read the pamphlet, I knew it was true. It had the address of the mission home; I made it there a few days later and asked for baptism. The Elders told me to just hold on, and gave me a Book of Mormon, with instructions to read it. Soon afterward I was drafted into the army and sent to Europe where I fought in the First World War. I was in the trenches and many times was close to death, but I read the Book of Mormon and the Bible continually and came home in good health.

As soon as I got home, I went to the mission home, and again applied for baptism. This time I was baptized and confirmed a member of the Church. The Holy Ghost was conferred upon me, but I didn't jump up and down and carry on. I asked the Elders if there was something I had missed, because I was not jumping. They informed me that such carrying on was not part of receiving the Holy Ghost, and asked me if I had a sweet warm burning in my heart and knew the Gospel was true. And I certainly did have a sweet calm assurance that it was all true.

Not long afterwards, as I was out working in the field, several men on horses came to me. They had guns and left me with the idea that they intended to use them. They told me:

Now look here nigger, you've been overseas and associated with white people and now you come home and join a white man's Church. You get right back down there and get your name off those books, and if you don't, we'll hang you to the highest tree and shoot you full of holes.

I was sure they would do just what they were threatening and went to the mission home and told the Elders of my problem. I looked for them to be concerned, but they just said, "Brother Hope, don't worry too much. It's only a little persecution."

Soon after this, I met my wife and she accepted the Gospel. It wasn't too long until we moved up to Cincinnati where we felt that we could serve the Lord better. [118]

A few years later the Hopes moved to Salt Lake City where Patriarch Eldred G. Smith gave them patriarchal blessings.

The Hope Family, circa 1936 (Len, Sr., Mary, Rose Ann, Izetta, Maryzell, Len, Jr., William, Vernon)

118.Words of Len Hope as recalled by Stanley L. Fish.

Church Leaders Visit the Branch

Although the Cincinnati Branch may have still seemed fairly small during this time, it was one of the pillars of the Northern States Mission. By the end of 1930, the Northern States Mission included 7,099 members, including "14 High Priests, 20 Seventies, 443 Elders, 226 Priests, 90 Teachers, 236 Deacons, 4,728 lay members and 1,342 children." Major chapels included the following:

> 2555 North Sawyer Avenue, Chicago (Logan Square Branch); at 6111 Kenwood Ave., Chicago (University Branch); at Indianapolis, Ind.; at Detroit, Michigan, and at Cincinnati, Dayton and Columbus, Ohio. Regular meetings were also held at Aurora, Decatur, Galesburg, Peoria, Rockford, Rock Island, Springfield and West Frankford, Ill.; at Evansville, Fort Wayne, Linton, Muncie, Peru, South Bend, Terre Haute and Vincennes, Ind.; at Ames, Boone, Davenport and Sioux City, Ia.; at Flint, Grand Rapids, Jackson, Lansing and Saginaw, Michigan; at Akron, Middletown, Portsmouth and Toledo, Ohio; and at Eleva, La Crosse, Milwaukee and Racine, Wisconsin.[119]

This put Cincinnati on the regular itinerary of Church leaders, allowing the branch to be visited by many apostles and other Church officials.

David O. McKay

In 1925, Ohio again became part of the Northern States Mission, which was then presided over by John H. Taylor. The Saints in Cincinnati still benefited, however, from their proximity to Southern States Mission. In 1926, David O. McKay, a member of the Council of the Twelve, was touring that mission with its president, Charles A. Callis, who later became a member of the Council of the Twelve. According to President Anderson, arrangements had been made to hold the East Kentucky District conference in Cincinnati, as had been the custom before Ohio's induction into the Northern States Mission. He described the conference as follows:

> Three meetings were held in our place of worship, Hall G, Odd Fellows Building, and all three sessions of the conference were crowded to overflowing.
>
> President David O. McKay was the main speaker at the three services. His sermons were intensely interesting. His pleasing voice and personality, his calm logical and convincing way in expounding the scriptures and the restoration of the Gospel made a deep impression upon the hearers, who listened with great attention and respect.

President Charles A. Callis thanked the Saints of Ohio, of which there was a large attendance, for their fellowship and loyalty, and exhorted them to be as faithful to President John H. Taylor as they had been to him. He bore a strong testimony to the truthfulness of the Gospel.

David O. McKay

---

119. Jenson, *Encyclopedic History of the Church*, 594.

A sumptuous luncheon was served on one of the large stages in the building between the first and second meetings in honor of the notable guests. The stage setting was a pretty garden scene, embellished with flowers and plants. Six large banquet tables were run longitudinally from the proscenium to the back of the stage, where a table, slightly raised, was placed crosswise for the guests. The tables were beautifully decorated with flowers, and tables for children were arranged in the "wings." The missionaries were grouped in the center. Upon the entrance of President McKay and President Callis, all seated at the tables arose and remained standing until they were seated. It was by far the most elegant and elaborate affair ever undertaken by the branch.

Heber J. Grant

Heber J. Grant

During the time Noah Pond was president of the Northern States Mission (1929-1931), Heber J. Grant, Prophet and President of the Church, visited Cincinnati. President Anderson wrote:

> Those who were there will never forget that meeting, nor the wonderful sermon he delivered. His humble, dignified bearing, intense sincerity, and powerful testimony about the restoration of the Gospel made a deep and lasting impression upon all.[120]

The next month during General Conference, Noah Pond said:

> The outstanding feature of our work during the last month was the visit of our dear President Grant, that we were favored with. He came into our mission and remained with us from February 16th to February 25th. During that time we had the privilege of dedicating the new chapel in Columbus, Ohio, and our beautiful chapel in the University branch in the city of Chicago; likewise visiting the chapel that had been completed during the past two years in the city of Detroit, where we have a beautiful building and a fine congregation of our membership, and active work. He also had the privilege of visiting our chapels and our congregations in Dayton and Cincinnati, Ohio, also Milwaukee, Wisconsin. Immediately following this visit a number of baptisms were performed. The saints and the missionaries will never forget the marvelous impression, the testimony, and the Spirit of the Lord that accompanied the visit of President Grant. We have been favored, since our entry into the mission with a visit from Apostle Ballard, likewise a tour of the mission by Apostle Orson F. Whitney. These brethren of the General Authorities of the Church are welcome. The saints, friends, investigators and missionaries will travel hundreds of miles for a single opportunity of meeting and hearing the words of inspiration that fall from the lips of the servants of God.[121]

120.Anderson, 7.

121.Noah S. Pond, *Conference Reports* (April 1930): 116.

Rudger Clawson

Another General Authority of the Church visited Cincinnati July 6, 1933. Rudger Clawson, then president of the Council of the Twelve, spoke in the Cincinnati Branch sacrament meeting. He was accompanied by Mission President George S. Romney. According to branch minutes, Elder Clawson told of his missionary experiences and how Elder Joseph Standing was murdered in cold blood while he and Elder Clawson were laboring together in Georgia. Elder Standing had a foreboding dream that indicated trouble. Two days later the Elders were accosted by an armed mob of twelve men who took them to an isolated spot. One of the men struck Elder Clawson from behind with a club and another fired a pistol at Elder Standing, mortally wounding him. They threatened to shoot Elder Clawson also, but in the end permitted him to go. After he left, they fired additional shots into Elder Standing's body. Elder Clawson retrieved the body and accompanied it back to Salt Lake.

James H. Wallis

James H. Wallis

Early in 1935, Patriarch James H. Wallis arrived and spent approximately two weeks meeting with the Saints in the Cincinnati area and giving many patriarchal blessings. Since there was no organized stake in the area and thus no patriarch, this was their first opportunity to receive the blessings. Patriarch Wallis was the grandfather of Budge Wallis, who later presided over the Cincinnati Ohio and Cincinnati Ohio North stakes. Patriarch Wallis kept a detailed journal that included entries about his stay in Cincinnati.

> Thursday, Jan. 31, 1935—We arrived [in Cincinnati] at 8:30. President Charles V. Anderson of the Cincinnati Branch, with two young men by the name of Bang, met us at the train and helped us to the hotel [Metropole].
>
> Sunday, Feb. 3, 1935—In the evening one of the brethren call for us to go to, meeting and he also brought us home again. Bro. Mathews and Mother [Patriarch Wallis's wife] went with me. It was a glorious meeting, and every member of the program was excellent. I spoke for 30 minutes. There were 20 more adults in attendance than at Sunday School.
>
> We enjoyed the testimonies borne at the fast meeting this morning. There were 27 who did so. There was a good spirit present, and more would have got up if there had been time.
>
> Monday, Feb. 4, 1935—Bro. Mathews and I took a taxi to the chapel, where I gave ten blessings. Met a lot of nice people during the day.
>
> Tuesday, Feb. 5, 1935—We got to the chapel at quarter to nine, and commenced giving blessings promptly at 9, and continued until 4 o'clock, without anything to eat.
>
> Wednesday, Feb. 6, 1935—Was at the chapel at 9 o'clock prepared to give blessings. Met the president of the South Ohio District, and his partner, Elder Gowers, and together we mapped out a schedule for our labors in this district, which includes Dayton, Xenia, Portsmouth, Hamilton and Middletown. We will hold public services in Dayton on Sunday after-

noon, at 2 o'clock and in Cincinnati at 6:30 at night. Elder Cahall came to our apartment in the evening and received his blessing.

Sunday, Feb. 10, 1935—Was up early this morning, as I have to speak this afternoon at 2 o'clock at Dayton, 52 miles from Cincinnati. The Dayton Branch is fortunate in having a fine chapel, which they own. There were about 45 or 50 people present. Bro. Mathews was the first speaker and I took up the remainder of the time.

Monday, Feb, 11, 1935—At 9 o'clock Pres. Thomas of the South Ohio District and Elder Reeves of Spring Valley Branch came to take Elder Mathews and I to give blessings at Dayton. It was 9:40 when we got there. It was much colder when we got there, and when we entered the church there was no warmth, the furnace fire not having been lit. The elders had prepared a small room about 6x8 for me to give blessings in, poorly lighted, and more poorly heated with a small gas heater with the fumes escaping into the room. We went to give blessings there but the fumes overcame us and we suffered headaches and nausea. It was impossible to stay there, so Elder Thomas secured us a room of one of the member's homes in which to finish our work. That got so cold that we could hardly do so. However, we remained and gave blessings to all scheduled and then left for home at about 3 o'clock.

Wednesday, Feb. 13, 1935—Gave a number of blessings this morning to members of the Church from Spring Valley, who traveled over 40 miles to get here. One was a sister 82 years of age. She appreciated the blessing very much. I gave the blessing in my apartment.

Saturday, Feb. 16, 1935—Spent all morning packing up and placing our apartment in shape, as we leave at 1 o'clock for Columbus, Ohio, 120 miles distant, where the North Ohio District Conference is to be held tomorrow.[122]

The Andersons Leave

On December 15, 1935, Branch President Charles V. Anderson gave his farewell address to the Saints in Cincinnati and bore strong testimony of the truth of the Gospel. Sixty-eight members were present. President Anderson had been a great teacher, a missionary, an organizer and a leader of youth and adults. After twenty-two years in Ohio, he had been called by the General Authorities of the Church to return to Salt Lake City.

As always when a leader of long standing and great stature leaves a calling, there were those who could not see how President Anderson could be replaced. During his stay, the branch had grown from a dozen members to more than two hundred. Most of these had known no bishop nor any other branch president and some placed confidence in him that was beyond even this great leader. A Sunday School teacher once pointed out to a class member that an opinion she was expressing was contradictory to certain passages

---

122.James H. Wallis, Diary, Cincinnati, Ohio, 31 January, 1935 -16 February, 1935. In possession of Gloria Wallis Rytting.

in the Doctrine and Covenants. "I don't care what it says in the D&C," she replied. "President Anderson said it was this way!"

A year and a half later, President and Sister Anderson were invited by the branch to return for a special six-month missionary assignment. It was a reunion of great joy. As President Anderson later wrote:

> Next day being Sunday we attended Sunday School in the chapel. And, oh, what a welcome! Old and young crowded around us; handshakes, embraces and tears of joy; even little children shouted our names and smiled. We had never thought of being received with such an outburst of genuine whole-heartedness by everyone. We shall never forget it, and if remembrance of happenings in this life goes with us into eternity, it shall have an outstanding place in our memory forever. The Sunday School Superintendency, Elder Robert Meier, Gus Mason, and Ray Chapin, showed us every courtesy, and I had the pleasure of addressing the Sunday School after re-assembling. The Sunday School is keeping up its reputation of being the best auxiliary in the branch. The teachers are capable, the order excellent, and the average attendance very large.[123]

During this visit Vernon Cahall recounted one spiritual experience with the Andersons:

> My wife was a member of the Church before me. About twelve years ago she had to undergo a serious major operation. Then general opinion at the hospital was that she would not recover. She told me to go to Brother Anderson, who was then President of the Cincinnati Branch, and ask him to come and administer to her. I did, and Brother and Sister Anderson went with me to the hospital. A large, white screen was put around the bed, and inside the enclosure was a nurse, besides us. President Anderson administered to my dear wife and promised her, in the name of Jesus Christ, that she would recover, and be out of the hospital in a couple of weeks. I looked at the nurse, and she smiled and shook her head. But Brother Anderson's prediction came true. My wife is with me here tonight, and in good health. I made a vow at the time, that if my wife got well I would join the Church, and I kept my promise. I have been happy ever since, for God gave me a convincing testimony that the Gospel is true.[124]

Charles Anderson passed away on September 26, 1952, and Sister Anderson joined him six years later on August 4, 1958. Of the Andersons, Ota Reeves wrote, "The Church has never known two more devoted saints.[125]

Charles V. and Christine Anderson, circa 1938

123. Anderson, 15.

124. Anderson, 27.

125. Ota Reeves, ed... "Historical Highlights of the Cincinnati Stake," Church Archives.

CHAPTER 4

A Pillar of the District
(1935-1958)

by Stanley L. Fish

President Anderson was a great teacher, a missionary, an organizer, and a leader of youth and adults. He did much to build up the Cincinnati Branch. Now it was time for other leaders to continue this work and for the Cincinnati Branch to help build up the Church in surrounding areas.

The Branch Moves On

In December 1935 the mantle of the branch presidency passed to Alvin B. Gilliam. He had been a counselor to President Anderson for over six years and was well prepared to take on the new calling as branch president when the Andersons left Cincinnati. He began his work with deliberation but soon moved into high gear. It would later be said of him that "he did more for the Church in Southern Ohio than any other person."

A.B. Gilliam

President Gilliam was a great supporter of the missionaries. One of his great desires was to make certain the missionaries had food, lodging, and transportation. Many times tears flowed from his eyes when, filled with the Spirit, he would tell about how the missionaries taught his mother the Gospel, about how he had been blessed, and about how, when he was a boy, his family had lacked so many of the world's goods but had been rich in having the Gospel.

President Gilliam was also a skilled salesman, one of those who could sell anything to anyone. He was a persistent and tireless worker and always willing to give, not only of his money but of himself. As branch president, he was with the Saints whenever they met in any capacity. If there was a cottage meeting, whether held by the traveling or local missionaries, he was there. Those who knew him best were his greatest supporters. He truly loved the Lord and as time went on Brother Gilliam came to be regarded as a great spiritual leader.

President Gilliam's counselors were dedicated, unassuming men who shouldered their part of the load. Christian Bang, Jr. had been but a boy when President Anderson first came to Cincinnati. Like President Gilliam, he was a generous man and greatly dedicated to the Lord's work. Vernon Cahall joined the Church in 1926 and had been faithful since. Each entry in the Cincinnati Branch Records from 1926 to 1936 was signed O. Vernon Cahall, Branch Clerk. After serving as President Gilliam's counselors, both men held many other callings. Vernon Cahall later became a bishop (Georgetown Ward) and patriarch of the Cincinnati Stake. Perhaps serving in this latter calling he was reminded of those days in early 1935 when visiting Patriarch Wallis noted the kindness that Vernon Cahall showed by providing him with transportation.

Brother Cahall's replacement as branch clerk was Henry Bang. The job then passed to Paul Bang, whose signature was on the branch records from 1936 to 1943. Like Vernon Cahall, Paul Bang was later called to be a bishop (Cincinnati Second Ward) and patriarch of the Cincinnati Stake and later the Cincinnati North Stake.

Under President Gilliam's leadership, the branch continued to grow. From July 1936 to November 1938 there were forty-nine baptisms recorded (some of these were children of record but most were new converts) and other people moved into the branch. This growth meant they were rapidly outgrowing the beautiful chapel, of which the saints were so justifiably proud. There was only a small room for a recreation hall and almost no classroom space.

Central Parkway YMCA

After much thought, study, and prayer, branch leaders decided to sell the building and try to build one that better suited the branch's needs. The Cincinnati Branch met at 216 Orchard Street for the last time on June 30, 1940. During the 110 years the Saints had been in Ohio, that was the only building the Church had owned in Cincinnati, the only meeting place the Saints had been able to call their own. Although leaving the building was a sign of growth, for many that was a sad day.

The following Sunday, the Cincinnati Branch began meeting at the Central Parkway YMCA. The Saints missed not having their own place to hold sacrament meetings, but were pleased to have extra classroom space. Even before they began meeting in the YMCA the branch performed its bap-

Bertha and A.B. Gilliam

tisms in the swimming pool. Baptisms were now more convenient—just a matter of walking downstairs. And the baptisms were quite frequent.

Central Parkway YMCA

In July 1939, Leo J. Muir became President of the Northern States Mission. Under his direction and under the leadership of President Gilliam, plans went forward to purchase land and construct a chapel. The following appeared in the Cincinnati *Times-Star*:

> A.B. Gilliam, 418 Highway Avenue, Ludlow Ky., president of the Cincinnati branch of the Church of Jesus Christ of Latter-day Saints (Mormon), said Thursday that the local mormon congregation had plans completed for a new $40,000 edifice at 47 East Hollister Street, Mt. Auburn, but the beginning of construction work was being delayed because of priorities on steel.
>
> Gilliam said the local group, now holding Sunday services in Central YMCA building, had a membership of approximately 400, scattered throughout the city. Several months ago it sold its church property on Orchard Street to the Immanuel Mission and purchased the homestead of the late August Garry Herrmann at the Hollister Street Address. The property had a frontage of 165 feet on Hollister Street and is 150 feet deep.[126]

General Authorities of the Church visited the area from time to time, but not on a regular basis. In January 1941, Richard R. Lyman of the Council of the Twelve had been in Dayton and many Saints from Cincinnati traveled there to hear him speak. In March of that same year, Oscar A. Kirkham of the First Council of Seventy spoke to the Saints in Cincinnati.

126.*Times Star*, March 6, 1941.

President Muir met with the Melchizedek Priesthood holders in the area on September 6, 1941, and discussed the problems associated with such a building. Eventually, with the outbreak of war, building materials became almost impossible to obtain and the project was set aside in favor of buying and renovating an existing structure.

In November 1941, Gilbert B. Ethington of Dayton was set apart as president of the South Ohio District. This was a milestone for the area in that President Ethington was the first called to that position who was not a traveling missionary and the Saints saw it as a first step in the direction of having an organized stake of Zion.

World War II

World War II not only slowed the construction of new church buildings, it also caused the Church's missionary force to be drastically decreased as well. But many of those young people who were now in the military were able to serve both their country and the Lord. They were not ashamed of the Gospel of Christ and sometimes this was difficult. One reported when he came home on furlough, "I am not too popular. My companions call me Holy Joe." An interesting report came from Daniel A. Blackwelder when he returned from Germany, where he had been a prisoner of war. He was once asked why, if he believed in God, he did not kneel and pray during the battle. He replied, "I've prayed all my life, night and morning. I have a continual prayer to my Father in Heaven. When it was time to fight, I had said my prayers and felt sure that my Heavenly Father wanted me to fight."

Among those that served in the military from the branch were Alva May Cook, Marion Wheeler, Robert Druck, Everett Hamby, Chester Hamby (who lost his life in the Solomon Islands), Clayton Blackwelder, Daniel A. Blackwelder, Victor Bang, and Samuel Bang. Merlin Fish, who entered the armed services elsewhere came here to live after the war. There were also many servicemen who were members of the Church from the West that were in Cincinnati at one time or another during the war.

Marion Hanks Serves in Cincinnati

Marion Hanks and Stanley Fish, 1942

In May 1942, Elder Marion D. Hanks (who was later called to the First Quorum of Seventy) was assigned to Cincinnati as a missionary. He baptized four people: Paul Hutchins Miller, Ray Miller (not the Ray Miller who later served as a bishop of the Cincinnati Second Ward), Alma Clair Goshen (now Mrs. Daniel W. Ryan), and Adeline Louise Stephen (now Mrs. Joseph Carey). Elder Hanks labored in Cincinnati and was then transferred. A few months later he returned as manager of a ladies sextet, consisting of sister missionaries: Louise Rae Peck, Merlene Grange, Myrtle Tolman, Iris Heaton (who later married Dan Blackwelder of the Cincinnati Branch), Felice Swain Smith, Marjorie McBride (who later married Dr. Reid Nibley, an accomplished musician himself and a professor at BYU).

According to Elder Hanks, this sextet gave 750 performances and appeared at seventy-five other denominations.[127] These six sisters did much to break down prejudice against the Church and were very well received by the citizens of Cincinnati. In fact James G. Stewart, the mayor of Cincinnati at the time, even helped deliver them in his official car to some of their appointments. After their mission, these sisters were offered commissions in the United States Navy if they would tour and boost the morale of the sailors who were still at war. The sisters declined even though this might have been helpful to their musical careers, feeling that their gifts were better used in more spiritual ways as they had during their mission.

Marion Hanks with the Sextet

Given their success, it is ironic that Elder Hanks originally turned down the job of being their manager. "My initial impressions were not highly favorable toward this kind of missionary work," Elder Hanks later wrote. "I thought it was entertainment, differentiated from 'real' missionary work."[128] In fact he was so strongly opposed to the idea that when his mission president asked him if he would be pleased to undertake this assignment, Elder Hanks replied that "No, I would not be pleased and I needed to know if this was an assignment or an invitation, in the latter case of which I graciously declined his offer."[129] His mission president, however, continued to push the idea and Elder Hanks was soon won over and was assigned with Elder Richins to the sextet. And once there, he did a fine job in organizing their appointments.

Elder Hanks did, however, make one modification to the sextet's way of doing things. He made sure that they accepted no invitation without it being understood that he was also to preach to the audience, that this preaching was an essential part of their program. In other words, as Elder Hanks later put it, "they were the anesthetic and I was the medicine."

127.Marion D. Hanks, personal letter to Brad Kramer, 22 April 1997.
128.Ibid.
129.Ibid.

Despite his serious approach, Elder Hanks was occasionally the object of some good-natured teasing. As he would walk down the sidewalk with six sisters following, he was asked if he were trying to rush the prophecy in Chapter 4 of Isaiah concerning seven women laying hold of one man.

Throughout the years Elder Hanks always felt a "deep love for Cincinnati and the most personal and memorable recollections of life there as a new missionary."[130] He was especially grateful to Christian Bang and his "angel wife," who "were as kind to [him] as anyone could be in this world." Of them he later wrote, "I have never known more generous or loving or devoted Latter-day Saints," and of all the members of the Cincinnati Branch he said that they still "remain cherished friends though circumstances have denied us the privilege of their frequent companionship."[131]

Along with Elder Hanks, the branch received missionaries from other parts of the country for many years, but in 1943, for the first time, the Cincinnati Branch was able to "export" missionaries. These missionaries were Virginia Abshire, Laverne Chapin, Dorothy Cahall, Victor Bang, and Adeline Taylor.

Christian Bang, Jr. and O. Vernon Cahall served as counselors to President Gilliam for more than six years. At a conference held May 31, 1942, they were released. On June 21, Stanley L. Fish was set apart as first counselor. On July 5, George Haslam—a man of great faith and talent who moved to Cincinnati from the West—became second counselor. Brother Haslam served for only six months before being transferred. On July 10, 1943, Paul Bang was set apart as second counselor to President Gilliam.

Although the Saints in Northern Kentucky were not within the boundaries of the mission responsible for the Cincinnati Branch, they continued to meet with the Cincinnati Branch. As their numbers grew, President James P. Jensen of the East Central States Mission decided to call upon the strength of the Church in Northern Kentucky and asked for a conference to be held in Covington under the direction of that mission. Sacrament service was dispensed with in Cincinnati that Sunday and the Saints from the Cincinnati Branch attended afternoon and evening sessions of the conference. Having met with the Saints of both places, President Jensen concluded it was best that the Saints of Northern Kentucky continue to meet with the Cincinnati Branch.

130.Ibid.
131.Ibid

The Branch Renovates a Synagogue

On October 22, 1942, the Saints purchased a building at 2524 Victory Parkway. The building had been a Jewish Synagogue and, although far from ideal for the branch's needs, it offered at least temporary comfort.

One major renovation had to be made before the building could be used. The floor in the center of the meeting area was raised several inches above the surrounding area. This was to accommodate the Jewish practice of providing separate areas for women to sit during worship. The nails were removed to reveal a beautiful maple floor the same height as that which was around it. The branch also contracted Janice Rebert, a roommate of Pat Gilliam's and a student at the Cincinnati Art Academy, to paint a painting of Christ behind the pulpit. The painting portrayed Jesus blessing a child and helping an older man and was extremely welldone.

Two who contributed greatly to this renovation project were Elmer Cox and Dewitt T. Corbin. They were not members of the Church, but they were skilled in what needed to be done and contributed many hours of labor. (Brother Corbin's wife was a member, however; and he joined the Church about 1980.) Other items needed changing but they had to wait for a more opportune time.

In the summer of 1944, further renovations needed to be made on the chapel. This was to be a priesthood project and a committee was selected, consisting of Julius Blackwelder, John Hanks, Paul Nichols, and Irvin Gibby. Brother Nichols and Brother Gibby were young men who were in Cincinnati working on PhDs.

The Victory Parkway Chapel

1. Jean Warfield
2. Brother Rampton
3. Sister Rampton
4. Unknown
5. Unknown
6. Unknown
7. Leila Lundquist
8. Unknown
9. Roy E. Lundquist
10. Wila Hamilton
11. Unknown
12. Lillian Theler
13. Unknown
14. Virginia Bang
15. Unknown
16. Unknown
17. James Bang
18. James Brooks, Sr.
19. Ralph Blackwelder
20. Unknown
21. Ronald Brooks
22. Unknown
23. Unknown
24. Anna Mae Sander
25. Scheeney Schautz-man
26. Victor Bang
27. Del Schautzman
28. Marylin Dunnsway
29. Elizabeth Roberts
30. Thelma Roberts
31. Del Roberts
32. Unknown
33. Milton Y. Taylor
34. Esther Taylor
35. Dale Kraft
36. Alma Mason
37. Delores Dunnaway
38. Ruby Sernok
39. Unknown
40. Unknown
1. Raligh Warfield
42. Unknown
43. Unknown
44. Rampton daughter
45. Charles E. Dixon
46. William Poe
47. Sister Poe

448. Stanley L. Fish
49. Ronald Taylor
50. Judith Fish
51. Valaria Schocky
52. Unknown
53. Lydia Stewart
54. Unknown
55. Unknown
56. Lee Meadows
57. Douglas Mackay
58. Unknown
59. Unknown
60. Unknown
61. Cornelius Brooks
62. Schnarrenerg
63. Unknown
64. Evelyn Meadows
65. Valarie Schocky
66. Unknown
67. Unknown
68. Lois Bang
69. Sam Bang
70. Ada Dixon
71. Don Blackwelder

72. James Brooks, Jr.
73. Garfield Sneed
74. Gary Broman
75. Julius Blackwelder
76. Elizabeth Black-welder
77. Christian Bang, Jr.
78. Jack Lundquist
79. Peaches Brooks
80. Norma Mason
81. Helen Mackay
82. Surnok girl
83. Unknown
84. Joey Dixon
85. Bill Poe's boy
86. Phil Dixon
87. Unknown
88. Unknown
89. Paul Bang
90. Edward J. Broman
91. Merlin K. Fish
92. Dunnaway
93. Unknown
94. Merlin V. Fish

95. Unknown
96. Surnok boy
97. Unknown
98. Sylvia Farris
99. Unknown
100. Paul Lowe, Sydney
101. Ruth Hill
102. Sister Dunnaway
103. Madge Schnarren-berg
104. Jerry Schnarrenberg
105. Adeline Taylor
106. Robert Broman
107. Unknown
108. Schautzman boy
109. Unknown
110. Rosa Bang
111. Unknown
112. Christian Bang, Sr.
113. Unknown
114. Norwood Druck
115. Unknown
116. little Sister Kramer
117. Henry Allard
118. Milisia Druck
119. Rhea Blackwelder
120. Janet Taylor
121. Unknown
122. Barbara Meadows
123. Unknown
124. Mildred Bang
125. Unknown
126. Sandra Bang
127. Unknown
128. Dennis Lowe
129. Unknown
130. Unknown
131. Unknown
132. Unknown
133. Rosalie Bang
134. Unknown
135. Dickey Meadows
136. Cindy Cordes
137. Unknown
138. Debby Cordes

139. Unknown
140. Kent Hamilton
141. Marshal Hamilton
142. Vicky Bang
143. Unknown
144. Lynn Hamilton
145. Unknown
146. Sam Bang, Jr.
147. Unknown
148. Steven Bang
149. Marlene Fish
150. Peggy Lowe
151. Doug Lowe
152. Melvin Fish
153. Diane Taylor
154. Sharon Blackwelder
155. Unknown
156. Linda Bang
157. Gary Fish
158. Rampton boy
159. Unknown
160. Jill Schnarrenberg
161. Unknown
162. Carma Lowe
163. Unknown
164. Mildred Litterral
165. Lois Fish
166. Jay Schnarrenberg
167. Louise Fish

With President Gilliam's encouragement, the entire branch soon became involved. President Gilliam brought a crew from work, which again included Elmer Cox and Dewitt T. Corbin. Sister Gilliam was Relief Society President, and she personally shopped for most of the material that went into the chapel. Because she did not drive, much of the shopping was done by bus or street car. A bad hip increased her difficulty in getting around. She spent many long days and long evenings getting things ready and supervising the sisters' in their participation in the project.

Renovations included a new driveway with concrete block walls on each side and concrete along the north side of the building. Inside, the basement was completely redone with a recreation hall, Relief Society room, kitchen, classroom, and restroom. These required new partitions, paint, lights, and flooring. The oak stairway leading to the chapel was finished. In the vestibule and chapel almost everything but the window frames was natural wood, and this needed to be sanded, filled, and varnished. It included hard white maple floors, oak pews, a new stand, and a new pulpit. Walls were plastered, new light fixtures were added, and the ceiling of stamped metal—about twenty feet above the floor—needed a lot of patching and paint. The ceiling and window frames were painted a soft ivory and the walls a Persian blue. The white maple floors were varnished and dark blue carpet was installed everywhere but in front and between the pews. The Saints were pleased with their work and proud of the new meetinghouse, which was to serve them for twelve years. When President Stoddard, president of the Northern States Mission, saw the building for the first time, he said, "There is not a meetinghouse in the whole Church more beautiful."

It turned out, however, that the work had been done without the prior approval of the Church Building Department. But when the Building Department heard how much had been done and that the branch was asking only for the cost of the materials, it either decided it was getting a real bargain or that the branch in Cincinnati was far enough from Church headquarters to be "judged outside the law." In any case, the branch had supplied the labor and the know-how and the Church paid the cost of materials.

About this time, the Church in Cincinnati began a period of growth. It affected not just the Cincinnati Branch, but other branches in the area as well. As World War II ended, the young people who had left Cincinnati to serve in the military returned as adults to establish families of their own. Those who were members of the Church were ready for leadership and those who were not were ripe for harvest by the missionaries. In addition, Saints from other parts of the country moved to Cincinnati in increasing numbers.

Creed Haymond Becomes Mission President

When David I. Stoddard was released after serving faithfully as mission president, he said he thought there would be a temple in Cincinnati because of its location. President Stoddard was replaced by President Creed Haymond. President Haymond was an athlete, energetic and full of faith. As he preached he would move from one side of the pulpit to the other so swiftly, with such fire and energy, that not one was surprised to learn he had been a competitive runner. He often drew upon his experiences as an athlete when addressing a congregation.

President Haymond was raised in Utah as a member of the Church. Once, on a birthday, he and his twin sister were in the company of Elder John A. Widtsoe, who told them they should set their minds to keep the Lord's commandments in the Word of Wisdom. The three made a pact that none of them would ever use tea, coffee, tobacco, or alcohol unless all agreed to it.

Later, while attending the University of Pennsylvania, Creed was captain of the track team and ran the 100-yard dash and the 220. In May 1919, his team and teams from all over the United States gathered at Harvard to compete in a national track meet. The night before the final matches, as Creed was preparing for bed, there was a knock at his door. It was his coach and he had a glass of wine.

"Creed, here is a little stimulant I would like you to drink. You and the rest of the team seem a little flat."

Creed respected his coach, but he knew he could not drink the wine. When the coach tried to insist, Creed remained firm. Finally the coach relented. He knew how much the Church meant to Creed and that Creed had trained well, but before leaving he warned that the other athletes were taking the "tonic" and that Creed had better not let the team down.

Left to himself, Creed thought about what he had been asked to do. Surely one small glass of wine would not harm him. But he remembered the pledge he had made to his sister and to Elder Widtsoe. With these things in his mind, he knelt to pray and asked the Lord to give him a testimony of the truthfulness of the Word of Wisdom.

He then went to bed and on that night he did not remain awake, tossing and thinking, as he often did. Rather, he fell asleep at once. Early the next morning, he was awakened by a knocking on the door. His coach was there, frantically enquiring about his health. When Creed said he had never felt better, the coach told him that every one of his teammates was ill and throwing up.

On the field that day, Creed won the trial run in the 100-yard dash and was set to run for the championship. In those days, runners dug holes in the track to use as starting blocks. When the starting gun sounded Creed pushed off, but the soil behind his foot gave way and he fell to his knees. Not being one to quit, he got up and began to run with all his strength. As he did so, he felt as if unseen hands were literally pushing him along. He passed all of the other runners, even the favorite, C.E. Johnson of Michigan. Creed Haymond was the winner.

When his next race was almost ready to begin, it was discovered he had not yet run the qualifying race and would have to do so. He had no difficulty qualifying but was then required to run the championship immediately afterwards, with no time to rest. In spite of protests, the race went on, but Creed need not have worried. He not only finished well ahead of his competitors but set a world record that was to stand until it was broken by Olympic star Jesse Owens in 1936.

The rest of the team, those who had taken the "tonic," did poorly or were unable to compete at all. That night Creed went to bed feeling quite comfortable with the day that had just passed. As he lay pondering, a voice—almost aloud—said, "Creed, have your prayers been answered?" President Haymond then told the Saints in Cincinnati that if anyone had ever hurried out of bed to kneel in thankful prayer, it was him. And he testified that "the Word of Wisdom is of God."

The Branch Helps Lead the District

Soon after the arrival of President Haymond, several changes took place. Brother Milton Taylor had been living in the Chicago area, serving as president of the Gary Branch. He returned to Cincinnati in 1946 and shortly thereafter succeeded Harry J. Russell as District President. A.B. Gilliam, who had been president of the Cincinnati Branch for eleven years, was his first counselor. His second counselor was Roy E. Lundquist, a stalwart member of the Church from the West. O. Vernon Cahall became district clerk.

The records indicate President Gilliam was released as branch president on February 2, 1947. He was succeeded by Stanley L. Fish, with Paul Bang as first counselor and Gus Mason as second.

Initially, three branches—Cincinnati, Hamilton, and Portsmouth—composed the South Ohio District. Instructions from President Haymond to the new district presidency were to concentrate on the youth, organize a district council, establish a district budget, and begin looking toward providing improved meeting facilities.

With the installation of President Taylor, the district leaders began earnest preparation to become a stake of Zion. A district Elders' quorum began to function and auxiliary organizations began to operate much as they might in a stake. Soon a district council was created. Members included Harry J. Russell, former district president and member of the Hamilton Branch; Enoch Rayburn, who had been serving as president of the Portsmouth Branch; and from the Cincinnati Branch Raymond Chapin, James Brooks,

Sr., William C. Young, Christian Bang, Sr., D. Allan MacKay, Gus Mason, Paul Bang, Merlin K. Fish, and Julius Blackwelder.

Stanley Fish, Christian Bang, Jr., and Milton Taylor

With so many of the district leadership (the district presidency, the district clerk, ten members of the district council, and various district auxiliary leaders) coming from the Cincinnati Branch, some may have wondered how it would survive. Paul Bang and Gus Mason had only recently been called as counselors in the branch presidency when they were released to serve on the district council. But this was a time of growth and the new demands put on the branch seemed only to accelerate that growth. Victor Bang returned to Cincinnati from a full-time mission and Andus Udell Blackham came to the University of Cincinnati to pursue a PhD. These men served in the branch presidency until the summer of 1952. Christian Bang, Jr. and Edward R. Broman then served until the release of the entire presidency in October 1953.

By the end of 1949 the Northern States Mission was divided leaving only three states—Ohio, Indiana, and Michigan. At that same time President Creed Haymond completed his mission and was succeeded by another able and willing servant of the Lord, President Carl C. Burton. President Burton was an active man who counseled leaders that if they always had a project of some kind going the members of the Church would grow from service.

In an effort to expand and strengthen the District, members of the District Council were assigned to serve as branch presidents or counselors or simply to attend and support the leadership in small branches. In January 1950, Paul Bang became the Branch President in Hamilton with Gus Mason as his First Counselor. Merlin Fish and Ray Chapin, Jr. were called as counselors to President Harold Hill of the Middletown Branch. At the time that branch was organized fifteen were present—six local members and nine representing the district. Christian Bang, Jr., his wife Mildred, and Brother O. Vernon Cahall travelled to Georgetown every Sunday for four years. Brother Cahall also served as Branch President in Chillicothe and later as Bishop in Georgetown. While he was serving there as Bishop, the Georgetown chapel was constructed.

During these years, stake dances and youth conferences were done in fine fashion under the direction of Julius Blackwelder and Helen Puckett. Gold and Green Balls and the New Year's Eve Balls were spectacular events with excellent professional orchestras. Eventually these dances were held in the Hartwell Country Club and were attended by as many as 400 people. Youth conferences were held in conjunction with the Central Ohio and Northern Ohio Districts and participation of 300 young people was not unusual. Particularly memorable was the 1953 trip to Palmyra for the Hill Cumorah Pageant followed by a testimony meeting in Cleveland.[132]

Revelers at a Gold and Green Ball
(Left to right: Milton Taylor, Esther Taylor,
Helen Taylor, Nelson Taylor, Harry Thieman, and friend)

The Cincinnati Branch, under the leadership of Stanley L. Fish, grew rapidly, and in 1953 its membership was approximately six hundred. At that time the many Saints in Northern Kentucky, who had been part of the Cincinnati Branch, were organized into a branch of their own. The first president of that branch was A.B. Gilliam and Roy E. Lundquist was first counselor. At that time Brother Gilliam and Brother Lundquist were also first counselor and second counselor in the district presidency.

That same year Paul Bang, Gus Mason, Merlin Fish, Ray Chapin, and O. Vernon Cahall were released from their callings in branch presidencies. Alan Hintze was called as branch president in Hamilton and Julius Blackwelder was called as branch president in Middletown.

132.Milton Taylor, "A Brief History of the South Ohio District," 1946 through 1953, unpublished manuscript, 54-55.

The Branch Builds a Chapel

With new growth came an old problem: space. Once again the Cincinnati Branch required a larger building. However, with World War II over, they could now build a building of their own. On January 15, 1955, the branch purchased property on 5505 Bosworth Place in Norwood for their new chapel. The property at that time was described as "a wilderness of trees and bushes."[133] This was all cleared by members over the next few months. The groundbreaking ceremony occurred on July 16, 1955, with George B. Hill, Roy E. Lundquist, and Paul Bang brandishing the spades. Construction began on September 1, 1955.

The Bosworth chapel cost $280,000 and required a great deal of donated money and, for a small branch, raising funds was a particular problem. The branch solved this problem partially by building a house for the Campbells at 8944 Blue Ash Road in Rossmoyne, which they then paid for, and by holding rummage sales, bake sales, Primary carnivals, dinners, dances, paper drives, mystery package sales, and "Waistline Measurements." One rummage sale alone, conducted by Carma Lowe, earned a thousand dollars for the building fund.

The Bosworth Chapel, 1958

In addition to branch members, others in the community helped out. The dedication booklet lists the names of fourteen firms who contributed to the building. These helped greatly, but mostly the donations came in the form of sweaty toil. The branch formed several crews to work on carpentry, landscaping, and other tasks. Members even took turns sleeping in the building at night to prevent vandalism. On July 4, 1957, fifty-seven men, a record, spent

133.Dedication booklet, The Church of Jesus Christ of Latter Day Saints, Cincinnati Branch, Evelyn Meadows, ed., p. 13.

their entire holiday working on the building. As the male members of the branch worked on the building, the sisters rotated the assignment to feed them. Chistian Bang, Jr., Roy E. Lundquist, Christian Bang, Sr., Milton Taylor, Julius Blackwelder, Louis Thieler, and Paul E. Lowe composed the building committee. The branch president at the time was Edward J. Browman with Merlin K. Fish as first counselor and Theodore A. DeRossier as second counselor.Capping years of hard work, Marion D. Hanks returned as a General Authority to dedicate the new Cincinnati Branch chapel on May 21, 1958. To commemorate the event, Margie Evelyn Meadows penned the following prayer:

> To Thee, our heavenly father
> We humbly dedicate
> This hallowed house of reverence
> A monument of our faith.
> We've labored hard to build it
> In worthiness of Thee;
> May it be ever brimming
> With Thy Spirituality.
> We ask Thee now to bless
> And ever consecrate
> This place unto Thine honor
> In which we congregate.
> May all who enter here partake
> Thy spirit's wakening call
> To love and serve and worship Thee
> Within Thy sacred hall.
> This fruit of all our labors
> In Jesus' name we give
> To Thee, and may we ever
> Within Thy presence live.
> Amen.[134]

The new Cincinnati Branch chapel became the home of not only the Cincinnati Branch, but also of the Southern Ohio District and, later on, the Cincinnati Stake.

134.Dedication booklet, The Church of Jesus Christ of Latter Day Saints, Cincinnati Branch, Evelyn Meadows, ed., p. 37.

CHAPTER 5

The First Modern Stake in Ohio (1958-1985)

By Wm. Budge Wallis

The creation of a Cincinnati Stake was something church members in the Cincinnati area had worked long and hard for. Its preparation began years before with the establishment of a district in southern Ohio and continued as the district organization gained experience and as the branches gained strength.

The District Prepares for Stakehood

On October 4, 1953, Lorin L. Richards, who had succeeded Carl C. Burton as Mission President, presided at a district conference where he released Milton Y. Taylor, A.B. Gilliam, and Roy E. Lundquist as the district presidency. They had served for nearly seven years. Roy E. Lundquist was sustained as the new district president with Stanley L. Fish and Thomas Staker as counselors and D. Allan Mackay as clerk.

Following Milton Taylor's lead, President Lundquist made the district's main objective to become a stake of Zion. This required a great deal on the part of the priesthood, the sisters, the young men, and young women to be able to operate as a stake. It also took more members.

For some time, southern Ohio had been operating independent of Dayton and other parts of central Ohio, but the lack of membership continued to be a stumbling block to the creation of a Cincinnati Stake. When President Taylor was released in October 1953, there were fewer than 1,100 Saints in the Southern Ohio District. But by the beginning of 1955, the membership of the district had reached 1,310, and the mission president asked President Lundquist for a list of those that could be recommended for leadership in a stake. On January 22, President Lundquist was released and Stanley L. Fish was sustained as district president with Milton Taylor and Charles E. Dixon as counselors.

The desire of members for a stake continued to intensify and on May 15, President Richards wrote the district presidency, asking, "Will you please send the names of the people who are living in our district in regard to the stake which we talked to you about?" On May 21, President Richards wrote again:

> We would appreciate having you send the names of the men you think would be good leaders in the proposed stake organization for South and Central Ohio. May we hear from you by return mail if it can be done, the answer to these three questions we have given you. Especially the one on forming a stake—we would appreciate getting that right back so we can get this information to the First Presidency.

But at this point, even the two districts together could not be made a stake. In October, however, the district boundaries were changed and the district increased in both area and membership. It then covered about two-thirds of Ohio, everything south from a line just north of Lima, and included not only what had been the South and Central Ohio Districts but also part of what had been the North Ohio District.

George B. Hill, counselor in the Great Lakes Mission presidency, was sustained as president of this newly created Ohio District. James Mortenson of Columbus was chosen as first counselor with Stanley L. Fish of Cincinnati as second counselor and Vern Bryson of Fairborn as district clerk. Each Friday night a presidency meeting was scheduled in Fairborn at Brother Bryson's home on Airway Road. President Hill would travel from Lima, Brother Fish from Cincinnati, and Brother Mortenson from Columbus. Each Sunday the presidency would visit one of the branches—Newerk, Athens, Dayton, Columbus, Portsmouth, or perhaps Zanesville.

This district was difficult to manage and unity did not really develop. There seems to be no record or recollection of a district conference ever having been held. The Saints in this area had, however, the chance to feel like a part of something big—at least part of something that covered a great deal of territory.

After a few months the northern portion of the district was reassigned and the remaining area was renamed the Western Ohio District. James Mortenson of Columbus was president, with Paul E. Lowe of Cincinnati as first counselor and T. Blair Evans of Dayton as second counselor.

The record is not clear, but in April President Mortenson was released and Thomas Blair Evans was set apart as president with Paul E. Lowe as counselor. This was the last change to be made before the long-awaited creation of the Cincinnati Stake.

As President Evans later wrote in his journal:

I didn't serve long with President Mortenson until the district was divided and I was called as President of the Western Ohio District. . . . It constituted about the Southwest portion of the state. District headquarters was in our only meetinghouse in Cincinnati, just 65 miles from our home in Dayton. The only other meetinghouse in the district was the one in Dayton. The Georgetown Branch met in a small building the members had constructed themselves, not under Church sponsorship. The Middletown and Covington branches met in large old homes owned by the Church. Springfield and Hamilton branches met in YM or YWCA's and the Fairborn Branch met in the Air Force Chapel on Wright-Patterson Field Air Base. Most of the members of that branch were military families stationed at Wright-Patterson. Most were officers.

Although my counselors and I were the only High Priests in the District, we had a fully staffed structure, including a district council. We were organized as a stake and the Mission President had us operate as though we were a stake. In fact, our instructions were to prepare ourselves to become a stake.[135]

The Cincinnati Stake Is Created

Apparently President Evans and the district followed those instructions well. On Saturday, November 22, 1958, Elders Mark E. Petersen and LeGrand Richards began interviewing brethren to lead the proposed stake. Thomas Blair Evans was called as the President of Cincinnati Stake. Paul E. Lowe was called as his first counselor and John A. Taylor as his second counselor.

Again from President Evans' personal history:

Mark E. Petersen and LeGrand Richards were given the assignment to organize the stake. They spent Friday night in our home in Dayton. They asked me to ask every member of the district council and branch presidencies and my counselors to meet with them on Saturday. On Saturday they interviewed each one of us. President Christensen called Saturday evening and asked Nola Jean [Sister Evans] and I to meet with the brethren later that night. Nola Jean knew all the time that I was to be the Stake President, but I did not. We were certainly humbled by the call. I was then asked to give names for my counselors, the High Council and Bishops by the next morning, which was Sunday. Obviously, I spent the night praying and selecting these brethren.[136]

The following day, Sunday, November 23, the actual organization of the stake took place. It was the first stake organized in Ohio since the organization of the Kirtland Stake in 1834 with Joseph Smith, Jr., as stake president. The Kirtland Stake was the first organized anywhere in this dispensation; the Cincinnati Stake was the 270th stake organized.

---

135. T. Blair Evans, Personal History, 31.
136. Ibid, 32.

It was a glorious day for many members of the stake. However it also stood out for other reasons, as President Evans later wrote:

> Sunday was a day long to be remembered. The stake was just organized and I was sustained as the first Stake President. A series of unusual events followed.
>
> Because of the long distances, it was our custom to have one of the branches provide a lunch for those who attended our quarterly conferences. We had a morning and an afternoon session and ate lunch in between. On this occasion the Hamilton Branch had been given the assignment to provide the lunch. They did so. They provided ham sandwiches and potato salad. One or the other was tainted. I suspect if was the salad because it was in a galvanized steel container. Not far into the afternoon session there were people leaving the chapel to go to the restroom. Then we could hear several who sounded like they were vomiting before they could get to the restrooms. Before the session concluded pandemonium reigned. People were lying down all over the meetinghouse, quite sick from food poisoning. Fortunately, we had two doctors who were members and in attendance. They diagnosed it as not a serious form of food poisoning, but most uncomfortable for a period of a few days. To this day we don't know which food caused it. One organization of the branch had prepared the ham sandwiches and another the potato salad. Each blamed the other. . . .
>
> Never-the-less, the organization of the stake continued. After the meeting, Elders Petersen and Richards set apart me and my councilors. Then Elder Petersen and I set apart all of the Bishops and Branch Presidents. Elder Petersen would not even let my counselors participate in this because they did not have the keys to give to Bishops and Branch Presidents. This was a lesson in church government for us. He had Elder Richards and my two councilors set apart all of the High Councilmen. Elder Petersen was quite ill from the tainted meal. He would have to run to the restroom frequently while ordaining and setting apart the Bishops and Branch Presidents. However, Elder Richards, even though much older, experienced no suffering. We would hear about this incident for years to come when we had visitors from the General Authorities.[137]

The new stake consisted of the Cincinnati, Dayton, Fairborn, Hamilton, Northern Kentucky, and Springfield wards as well as two independent branches in Georgetown and Middletown.

A stake patriarch was not called at this time and Saints who wished to receive their patriarchal blessings had to go to Detroit, where Brother Reed Andrews served as Patriarch, or to Salt Lake City, where Church Patriarch Eldred G. Smith might give them a blessing.

At least one of those counselors that President Evans was inspired to select was extremely surprised. John A. Taylor was then just thirty years old and had been in the area just over two years. He had been called as a counselor to President Lundquist six months before.

137.Ibid, 32-33.

As John A. Taylor writes in his personal history:

> I was very startled to be interviewed by Elder Petersen, and could not have been more surprised to be selected as President Evans's Second Counselor. As Elder Petersen presented the names for a sustaining vote, and mine was read, Catherine and I were seated way back in the congregation. A woman just in front of us turned to her companion and said in a very loud voice: "WHO'S John Taylor!?" She seemed considerably embarrassed when a minute later Elder Petersen asked me to come to the stand, and I rose right behind her seat. Through the years when I show a lack of humility, Catherine will say to me: "WHO'S John Taylor?" Works every time.[138]

Blair Evans Establishes the Foundation

President T. Blair Evans was at that time a high-ranking industrial engineer at Wright-Patterson Air Force Base, located near Fairborn, Ohio, where he lived. Paul E. Lowe, the first counselor, was a very successful engineer in General Electric's jet engine facility near Cincinnati. Paul lived in Blue Ash, while John Taylor as a media supervisor with Proctor and Gamble and lived northeast of Cincinnati in Silverton.

President Evans traveled extensively throughout the stake, wearing out several automobiles during his administration. There was no interstate expressway linking Cincinnati and Dayton, for example, so he had to make use of an assortment of small highways, which rise and fall, twist and turn through small towns and hamlets. Driving was dangerous at all times, especially late at night, or in bad weather, and fatigue was always a companion, as President Evans describes:

> Because both of my councilors lived in Cincinnati, we held most of our presidency meetings there. We met in one another's homes, as we did not have stake offices. Although the Cincinnati meeting house was where we held stake conferences and High Council and Stake leadership meetings, there was no office for the Stake Presidency. If we needed an official office for sensitive business, we would use the bishops office. I drove at least 1000 miles each month either between Cincinnati and my home in Dayton, and visiting the far flung wards and branches. Adding to this were the weekly stake auxiliary meetings and weekly High Council meetings, all held in Cincinnati, some 75 miles from my home. I had been schooled to hold frequent leadership meetings, having grown up in the old Ogden Stake, where such a practice had actually been started by my own grandfather, Thomas B. Evans, who was the first president of that stake.[139]

Not only was distance and travel a challenge, but the task of teaching and training was a huge task as President Evans explains:

> As the presidency of the new stake in an area where few members had experienced the strength and administration of the church, we had some

T. Blair Evans

138. John A. Taylor, Personal History.
139. Evans, Personal History, 34.

great challenges. We had the task of teaching church administration. My goal was to solidify the members in the faith. In today's admonition, our mission was to perfect the saints. This we did with unusual emphasis on teaching church government and administration. We held seminars, first with the High Council, then with all the bishops. We taught not only church government and administration of the programs, but also the principles of effective leadership. I used much of my knowledge and training in the management field to prepare and conduct these seminars. We were pleased with the results. I found out later that I was regarded as a stern leader. I guess this was true because I insisted we all thoroughly study the various manuals published by the church and conduct our programs as closely as possible to those manuals. I would not permit deviation of the following of old sectarian practices learned in other churches before joining the true church.[140]

The high priests and seventies quorums grew rapidly in numbers and in strength. Within the first four months some 25 Seventies and 33 High Priests were ordained.

Immediately the new stake presidency began work on what it saw as the most urgent need in the stake—buildings.

During the next five years we constructed and dedicated six meeting-houses. The first was in Springfield, Ohio. The property for this building had been donated by a non-member who had known some faithful members of the Church while serving with them in the war. He was so impressed that he donated the property. Next was the building in Fairborn, Ohio. This building was dedicated by President Marion G. Romney, of the First Presidency. . . . The next building dedicated was in Middletown, Ohio. This was half-way between Cincinnati and Dayton so we began to hold many of our stake meetings there, which cut down on travel distance and time for many of us. The next was the Covington Chapel in Northern Kentucky. Next was the Georgetown Ward in Georgetown, Ohio. The last was the Hamilton Ward in Hamilton, Ohio.[141]

In March 1959, Elder Marion D. Hanks of the First Council of the Seventy, presided at the first conference since the organization of the stake. He was accompanied by Arben O. Clark, coordinator of the General Church Welfare Program. Elder Hanks found a warm welcome from the Saints, many of whom had known him when he labored in Cincinnati as a missionary or remembered when he had dedicated the Cincinnati Branch chapel.

During one of the leadership meetings of this conference, each of the leaders who spoke emphasized the importance of his call and his organization. Bishop Lundquist of the Cincinnati Ward observed that "each of these different auxiliaries seems to be the most important and to take precedence." He then asked Elder Hanks, "Which one should be stressed the most?" Elder Hanks replied, "The way I understand it, it just depends on which one you're responsible for."

140.Ibid, 39-40.
141.Ibid, 36.

At another stake conference not long after the stake was organized, Elder Harold B. Lee ordained and set apart Elder Harry J. Russell of the Hamilton Ward as the first patriarch of the Cincinnati Stake. For the first time since James H. Wallis had visited Cincinnati twenty-four years before, patriarchal blessings could now be given here. In addressing the conference, President Lee pointed out that the blessings promised by a Patriarch may not always come in mortality but may well be granted in the spirit world.

He also spoke of how men could come to magnify their priesthood callings. He compared working in the priesthood to being part of a team of horses. One might be a steady, seasoned horse and the other a bronco with no experience. When the two horses worked together the seasoned horse pulled when pulling was needed and held when it was necessary to hold. Eventually the inexperienced horse learned to do the same. Brother Lee noted that in the same way as new brethren worked with experienced brethren, they became "Priesthood broke."

On September 6, 1959, the Georgetown Branch become a ward. O. Vernon Cahall was called as bishop with Thomas L. Knott and P. Winton Reichardt as counselors and James A. Ratliff as clerk. This was a joyous occasion, but it also presented a challenge for President Evans:

> In the process of sustaining the bishop, about thirteen members held up their hands, opposing the sustaining of their bishop. I immediately stopped the sustaining and asked to meet with each of these members after the meeting. This I did far into the night, and I was about 130 miles from home. As I interviewed each of these members, most of them sisters, I found not a single charge that would not make the brother worthy of being their bishop. The complaints were largely that the bishop had not recommended the sisters' husbands to be advanced in the priesthood as soon as he had others. Petty reasons similar to this were given. None questioned the bishop's moral worthiness or testimony, these being the only reasons one should not be sustained. This I explained to them. The next Sunday I drove all the way back and again asked the ward members to sustain their bishop. They did so unanimously.[142]

On September 12, 1959, Bellefontaine became a dependent branch and part of the Springfield Ward. George N. Cloud was called as branch president. Sydney, Ohio, also had a dependent branch presided over by President Michael Bennet.

Some of the smaller branches were still in need of outside help. Merlin Fish and Raymond Chapin had been assigned to Middletown for a number of years before there was a stake. Julius Blackwelder was still assigned there when the stake was created but was released in May 1960. At that time John Zachrison, then a member of the high council, was installed as branch president. With the hard work of the Middletown Saints and the help of brethren from other parts of the district, that branch began to grow. Even at this early date, there was talk of a branch in West Union that would be dependent on the Georgetown Ward.

142.Ibid, 39.

President Harold B. Lee sent a letter that was read to the high council November 4, giving permission to make two wards from the Cincinnati Ward. On December 4th, Elder N. Eldon Tanner, then an assistant to the Twelve Apostles, presided over a quarterly conference at which the Cincinnati Ward was divided. Bishop Roy E. Lundquist was released as were his counselors, Milton Y. Taylor and Clifford Clive. Merlin K. Fish was set apart as Bishop of the Cincinnati Ward, with Charles E. Dixon as first counselor and Curtis L. Hamilton as second counselor. Paul Bang was set apart as the Bishop of the Cincinnati Second Ward, with Clifford Clive as first counselor and Homer R. Forbes as second counselor. The division became effective at the first of the year.

By March 5, 1961, the population of the stake had grown to 2,920. At a conference on that date, names of twenty-two Cincinnati Stake "home missionaries" were read.

On May 14, 1961, the Wilmington Dependent Branch was formed for the members of the Fairborn Ward residing in the Wilmington area. Lloyd M. Munsen was called as president of the new branch. On February 25, 1962, the Springfield Ward was transferred to the newly organized Columbus Stake.

Two brethren from the Church Genealogical Committee, Elder Zelph Y. Erickson and Donald M. Bagley, attended the stake conference on May 18-19, 1963, holding meetings with the Saints and leaders on Saturday. The presiding General Authority was Elder Henry D. Taylor, Assistant to the Twelve Apostles.

From President Evan's journal:

> I do not consider myself a spiritual giant in any sense of the word and have not had many of the spiritual experiences related by many saints . . . . [But w]e were holding a Stake Conference in Cincinnati. Our visitor was Elder Taylor, of the First Council of the Seventy. He headed the Church Welfare program and had come not only as our visiting General Authority, but also to organize a new Welfare Region, consisting of the Cincinnati, Columbus, Indianapolis and Ft. Wayne Stakes. We met Saturday afternoon and he effected the organization. I was called to be Chairman of the Welfare Region. James Mortenson, whom I knew very well and love dearly, was President of the Columbus Stake. I had served as his counselor in the Presidency of the Ohio District prior to the organization of the Cincinnati and the Columbus stakes. We went home that evening and I prepared for Stake Conference to be held next morning. Very early in the morning I received a telephone call from a councilor in the Columbus Stake presidency. He was in Wilmington, Ohio. On their way home to Columbus Saturday evening, they had had a terrible automobile accident. President Mortenson was in critical condition in the hospital, with severe head injuries. He was not expected to live. I immediately arose, dressed and started out of the drive towards Wilmington. It was somewhat out of the way towards Cincinnati and I told Nola I would go on to Cincinnati and they should come to the conference in the other car. On the way to the hospital, I reflected on the great life of President Mortenson and how he had been a Godsend to the saints in this area. Surely the Lord would spare him so he could continue his marvelous and necessary leadership. Never

in my life had I felt so strongly that I should walk into the hospital, go to his bedside and command him in the name of the Lord to be healed. I arrived at the hospital and walked to the entrance still feeling I should exercise the priesthood to heal him. As soon as I entered the hospital, that very real feeling immediately left. It was a very real feeling. I knew President Mortenson would die and we were not to try and keep him. He did pass on shortly thereafter. I have never forgotten that feeling which came over me. I know the Lord does call some of His choice servants home to perform greater callings even though it would seem to us their calling here is almost irreplaceable.[143]

A great effort was made at this time to educate the Saints and enhance the missionary work, and many signs of growth were evident. *The Windows of Heaven*, a film on tithing, was shown in every ward and branch. In Georgetown, ground was broken for a new chapel on June 23, 1963, just west of the city on Route 125.

A five-stake youth conference was held at Miami University, Oxford, Ohio. It was attended by 583 people, of which 184 were from the Cincinnati Stake. Sister Thomason from the MIA General Board spoke.

In July, the stake held a special fast to strengthen both the members and the missionary work. Two meetings were held especially for investigators, one in Fairborn and one in Cincinnati. Approximately four hundred people attended. In August, Dr. Hyrum Andrus and Professor Ivan J. Barrett of Brigham Young University held a seminar on Joseph Smith. Held in Dayton, 370 people attended the seminar.

At the September 1963 stake conference, President Evans presided. John Taylor had been assigned to speak in the morning session. An interesting thing happened, which greatly amused the congregation and demonstrated the quick wit and dry sense of humor that was characteristic of President Evans. The incident was reported by J. Paul McGregor—a member of the Northern Kentucky Ward and a long-time resident of Cincinnati, who had a wide circle of friends in the community—to Si Cornell, *Cincinnati Post & Times Star* newspaper columnist.

On September 19, a few days after conference, the following appeared in Cornell's column:

> Every three months, about 1,000 local Mormons gather in a big conference. John Taylor, a Procter & Gamble advertising man for Crest and other products, addressed the most recent meeting. He spoke from the Old Testament about Daniel, Shadrack, Meshach and Abednego.

> John told how the four had refused the royal meats and wines of King Nebuchadnezzar over a period of time in preference to a simpler diet. At the end of this test period the four were adjudged healthier than those who partook of the king's bounty. John concluded his talk by reading a note which had been passed to him by the conference president [T. Blair Evans]. The note read: 'Which group had the fewest cavities?'[144]

143.Ibid, 37-38.
144.Taylor, Personal History.

This question caused great laughter among the congregation. Most readers of these words will remember that the question President Evans asked, was the foundation of Crest's massive advertising campaign for many years.

The stake conference held December 1-2,1963, was five years and one week after the creation of the stake. The visitors were Elder Gordon B. Hinckley of the Council of the Twelve and John K. Edmunds and D. Arthur Haycock of the General Priesthood Committee. At the Saturday night session, Elder Hinckley directed his remarks toward "Overworked Bishops" and the importance of delegation.

In the Sunday afternoon session, conducted by President T. Blair Evans, it was proposed and sustained that a new ward, the Kettering Ward, be created from parts of the Dayton and the Fairborn wards. Roger Nielson was sustained as bishop of the new ward. Roy E. Lundquist was sustained as Patriarch of the Stake.

On September 6, President Evans and his counselors, President Lowe and President Taylor, organized the Middletown Branch into the Middletown Ward. Elder Lynn James Boulter was set apart as bishop, with Charles A. Rolph as first counselor and Leon Wolford as second counselor.

The creation of the Middletown Ward was indeed a milestone. The little branch had struggled for many years and many from other parts of the stake had worked to help it grow: John Zachrison from Dayton, Julius Blackwelder and Merlin Fish from Cincinnati, and Ray Chapin from Northern Kentucky.

Just a week after the Middletown Branch became a ward, the stake presidency was changed for the first time. Paul E. Lowe was released as first counselor and John A. Taylor, who had been second counselor, became first counselor. Herbert B. Spenser became second counselor. Elder Thomas S. Monson of the Council of the Twelve was the General Authority who made the change. With him was Lorin F. Wheelwright of the General Sunday School Board.

On September 27, 1965, Patriarch Roy E. Lundquist passed away with a heart attack while at work. He was survived by his wife, Leila C. Lundquist of the Cincinnati Ward, two sons, and one daughter. Elder Lundquist was nationally known for his work in flood control with the Corps of Engineers. He had been in the Cincinnati area for more than twenty years and had been a tireless worker. He had held almost all branch callings and almost all district and ward callings, including Sunday School superintendent, high councilor, and stake patriarch.

The Cincinnati Stake grew from some 2200 to some 2800 members in the first six years. At this time it was proposed to the brethren in Salt Lake City to organize a Dayton stake. President Evans was even authorized to purchase property for a stake center in the Dayton area. However, the brethren told the stake that it was not quite ready for such a division.

John A. Taylor Educates the Saints

At the stake conference held January 29-30, 1966, Elder Mark E. Petersen of the Council of the Twelve once again presided. With him was William J. Critchlow, Assistant to the Council of the Twelve. At this conference, Elder Petersen released President Evans along with his counselors, John A. Taylor and Herbert W. Spencer. President Evans later explained what caused this:

John A. Taylor

> I was released as Stake President by Elder Mark E. Petersen, who had called me. I had changed employment, going to the IRS, necessitating our moving. I remember calling Elder Lee on the phone and joking with him that the IRS was after me. He didn't even chuckle, thinking the worst had happened. After I explained to him what I was offered, he said I would be given an honorable release and did not discourage me from going with the IRS. I had told him I would not accept their offer if he felt I should stay with the stake.[145]

Of President Evans, John A. Taylor wrote:

> T. Blair Evans was a dedicated and tireless leader. He travelled extensively throughout the stake, wearing out several automobiles during his administration. It should be noted that the Cincinnati Stake extended from Sidney and Bellefontaine on the north, to Walton in Northern Kentucky on the south, a distance of around 125 miles. The stake also extended from the border of Ohio and Indiana on the west, to Georgetown and beyond on the east, a distance of near 100 miles. Over country roads this was by any measure an enormous geographic area to cover, actually over 12,000 square miles.[146]

Elder Petersen then called John A. Taylor, who had been a counselor to President Evans since the stake was formed, as the new stake president. President Taylor asked Gerald L. Scott to be his first counselor and Henry Heilesen to be his second counselor. O. Vernon Cahall was set apart as stake patriarch.

> Concerning his counselors, President Taylor wrote:

> Gerald Scott, originally from Washington DC, had recently moved to Cincinnati, and was chief executive of the local plant of a major national baking company. He was very new in our area, but I'd had an interview with him for some reason or other, and recognized that he was a personable and effective leader. For that reason I felt very comfortable about requesting that he be called as my 1st Counselor even though we were barely acquainted. I'm sure the Lord brought him to Cincinnati to be available for this appointment! President Scott is a brother of Elder Richard G. Scott [of the Quorum of the Twelve].

> Henry Heilesen was employed by the White Paper Division of the Mead Corporation headquartered in Dayton. I don't recall how we became acquainted, but I wanted a counselor in the north end of the stake, and

---

145. Evans, Personal History, 41.
146. Taylor, Personal History.

Henry was a natural choice. Not too many years before he had been student body president at Brigham Young University. He was a keen and diligent leader.[147]

On the second day of June that same year, a branch library of the Genealogical Society was opened in Cincinnati. *The Fairborn Daily Herald* carried an informative article about the new branch library, explaining that all genealogical seekers, whether or not they were LDS, would be able to use it.

One of the great benefits of the new Bosworth chapel was enough room for a genealogical library. This was a late addition to the building, made possible when the branch received a donation of over a hundred books dealing with genealogy and local history from Marie Dickore, a local historian. Continuing its entrepreneurial spirit, the branch held more bake sales and a rummage sale to help equip the library. When it opened, it had just one microfiche reader.

Stanley L. Fish was the first chairman of the Genealogical Society with Ross Massie and Carl Plummer succeeding him. Harriet Plummer served as an assistant librarian.

The records indicate the first time General Conference was televised in Cincinnati was April 8, 1967. Both WHIO-TV in Dayton and WKRC-TV in Cincinnati carried the conference. General conferences continued to be carried on and off the Cincinnati and Dayton areas for the next ten years.

On January 27-28, 1968, Cincinnati Stake conference was held with Elder Marion G. Romney of the Council of the Twelve Apostles as the visiting General Authority. At this conference, the bishoprics of the Cincinnati Second and Northern Kentucky wards were reorganized. Enfred J. Lundberg replaced Paul Bang as bishop of the Cincinnati Second Ward and Crafton Grant Chapin replaced Robert Ginn as bishop of the Northern Kentucky Ward. Also, the Cincinnati Third Ward was created from parts of the Cincinnati Second and Hamilton wards.

The new Third Ward took in the northeast corner of Hamilton County. Ronald C. Baum was set apart as Bishop with Stephen B. Affleck as first counselor and John C. Black as second counselor.

On January 12, 1969, President John A. Taylor reported on his visit to the Washington DC temple site and on the meeting held there with President N. Eldon Tanner presiding. At the meeting, the stake presidents were invited to help decide on the design of the temple and on how the cost should be allocated to the stakes in the temple district.

> For quite some time I had been making regular trips to Washington, DC, as a member of the Temple Committee. Eventually, N. Eldon Tanner, Second Counselor to President David O. McKay, met with representatives of the stakes on the eastern seaboard and south, central, and north stakes in the proposed new district. It was most interesting, as he did not come among us with a hard and fast proposal for the size or cost of the Temple. The site, on a forested hilltop had been fixed. Though the meet-

147.Ibid.

ing with Elder Tanner was in a chapel, he was quite informal, and asked for personal opinions. This discussion continued for several hours during which time a general view was shaped as to the desired size, amenities and cost of the proposed Temple Project, based on what we thought could be obtained within a large chunk of the country, roughly from the midsection to the east coast, there not being a temple west of Salt Lake City at that time. I reported progress on the Temple Project to our priesthood leaders at appropriate times and to the members at stake conference.

Eventually a budget was set and the costs were allocated to each stake based on population. On February 13, 1969, at a Stake Presidency and Bishoprics Meeting, I presented this project for discussion. Stake and ward leaders sustained the project; it was carried to the members, and fund-raising began. Within the Cincinnati Stake we divided the Washington Temple assessment among our wards and branches based on membership weighted by financial ability (demonstrated by tithepaying). Many wonderful stories of commitment and sacrifice were later reported by our bishops. Needless to say, our portion of the funds was raised by the deadline.[148]

February 22-23 stake conference was held, with Elder LeGrand Richards of the Council of the Twelve presiding, assisted by Edwin B. Jones, regional representative; and G. Garret Barlow, Ohio Mission President. Paul Bang was set apart as stake patriarch.

Deseret News article reporting the Cincinnati win

In March 10-15, 1969, the All-Church Basketball Tournament was held in Salt Lake City. The Cincinnati First Ward team consisting of Mel Fish, Stan Fish, Randy "Hollywood" Wardwell, Randy Harkness, Jerry Sink, and others won the tournament and the sportsmanship award. Melvin G. Fish was chosen as the most valuable player. This was the first time a team from east of the Mississippi had ever won and one of the few times the first place team also took the sportsmanship award. The team was most pleased with the sportsmanship award and displayed the trophies in the foyer of the Bosworth

---

148.Ibid.

Place chapel for many years.Several quarterly conferences were held in places other than the stake center because the attendance was too high for the Church-owned buildings. Conferences were held in the Norwood and Princeton high schools.

Prior to the stake division, conferences were held in Lemon-Monroe High School near Middletown, as it was equal distance between Dayton and Cincinnati. On February 22, 1970, a stake conference was held there, with Elder Theodore M. Burton presiding. On that occasion President Gerald L. Scott was released (he was moving from the Cincinnati area to accept a new management position). Henry Heilesen was sustained as first counselor, and Leo P. Vernon as Second Counselor. Leo was at that time Director of the Charles Kettering Research Laboratory in Yellow Springs (Antioch College's home town), and probably the world's foremost authority on the subject of Chlorophyll. He was formerly bishop of the Fairborn Ward.

A social event everyone looked forward to was the annual Bishops' Ball. President Evans began a tradition, which President Taylor followed, which was to pay for hosting a banquet for the bishops out of the small stake president's allowance provided by the Church for travel, postage, etc. On such an occasion, December 14, 1968, in a private meeting, the annual stake budget was presented to the bishops for their sustaining vote. Then we adjourned for a banquet with their companions. Alma Ryan, Stake Relief Society President, was famous for managing the food aspects of this event. The dinner was followed by the "Bishop's Ball," to which all stake members were invited. A tally was kept of attendance by ward, and during the floor-show the bishop with the greatest ward attendance (based on percentage of members) was feted and crowned. On this particular occasion Elder Edwin R. Jones, our Regional Representative, was on hand for the entire evening.

One of the outstanding social events in the history of the stake took place on November 21, 1969. Throughout the Church, stakes were encouraged to plan for a "Centennial Ball," commemorating the 100th Anniversary of the organization of the YWMIA. The Young Men and Young Women organizations threw their energies behind making this a highly memorable event. One of the young leaders, Merlin V. "Tiny" Fish, had very expansive ideas about this event, and as the result of his vision and enthusiasm, the formal dance was held in the grand ballroom of Cincinnati's beautiful Sheraton-Gibson Hotel, and was extremely well-attended. Many men in the stake, young and old wore tuxedos probably for the first (and maybe last) time!

At stake conference on May 23 and 24, 1970, Elder Mark E. Petersen, and Elder Roy W. Oscarson, the Regional Representative at that time, organized from the Cincinnati Stake, the new Dayton Stake, consisting of the following units: Dayton, Fairborn, Kettering, Middletown, Piqua Branch from the Cincinnati Stake; Springfield Ward, and Bellefontaine Branch from the Columbus Stake, and the Connersville Branch from the Indianapolis Stake. Joseph M. McPhie, an Air Force Colonel, was appointed Dayton stake president.

The new abridged Cincinnati Ohio Stake then comprised the Cincinnati First, Cincinnati Second, Cincinnati Third, Georgetown, Hamilton, and

Northern Kentucky Wards, and the Wilmington Branch. Since he had recently moved to the Cincinnati area from Dayton, Henry Heilesen continued as first counselor to President Taylor. Enfred J. Lundberg was called as second counselor.

Due to the tremendous leadership pool provided by the Wright-Patterson Air Force Base, both military and civilian, the Dayton Stake was considerably stronger when divided out. But the long-term results for both stakes were highly beneficial in every respect, as President Taylor later wrote:

> I recall our difficulty, in the highly truncated Cincinnati Stake, in rebuilding our high council and stake auxiliary organizations as so many of our leaders had been provided from the north. Of course, under the best of circumstances the wards and branches had to bear the brunt as we took so many leaders from their midst. But this is development, as local replacements grow to fill the gaps. Then too, when relatively inexperienced individuals serve in stake positions, they become strengthened in their abilities and are more effective when returned to their local units.
>
> During the many years of my administration, the stake presidency was focused on building-up the faith of the people, strengthening leadership at the local level, establishing strong priesthood and auxiliary organizations at the stake level, and implementing new Church programs. We continued the development of the Branch Genealogy Library, originally established by President Evans. During those years the Correlation Program, formal Teacher Training Program, Meeting House Library Program, a host of changes in youth programs, and other substantive auxiliary and other programs were announced, and we worked very hard to implement them throughout the stake as quickly as possible. The Regional Representative level within the General Authorities was inaugurated, and we had many very effective individuals assigned to us over the years, Elders John K. Edmunds, Ed Jones, Roy Oscarson, and Bob Barker quickly come to mind.[149]

As growth took place in the Cincinnati Second Ward, it was felt that a group of members living on the west side of Cincinnati would better be served by forming a dependent Sunday School. This was done on May 15, 1971, and Howard C. Brooks was called as president. A year later, May 14, 1972, the Cincinnati West Branch was created and Noel E. Winn was called as branch president. The branch met in the Westwood town hall and soon members from southeastern Indiana started meeting with them.

Tom and Marie Knott were staunch members who lived in Hillsboro. Their support was very important in the development of the Georgetown Branch and Ward, and the Wilmington Branch. Tom served in many ward and stake positions, and Marie is one of the area's leading genealogists.

149.Ibid.

Tom was acquainted with a Turner family who owned a large tract of land, mostly forested, near Folsom, Ohio, not far from Hillsboro. The Turners had heard good reports of the youth programs and generously invited the Church to make use of their undeveloped land for the youth activities, as President Taylor explains:

> Some preparations were necessary as there were no improvements, such as water, electricity, etc., on the property. Many individuals helped with this work, including one great occasion when the Stake Presidency and High Council assembled one Saturday with shovels, wheel barrows, etc. One recollection of the day is strong with me, as I dropped a major rock, breaking a toe. This did not hinder or halt the work. Over a fairly short time, a rough road had been cut down into the property which was essentially a valley with a high rim. The road, dug into Ohio clay, was extremely steep, and absolutely non-negotiable when wet. On the rim we established a parking lot for about ten vehicles, a large portable water tank and hundreds of feet of garden hose to provide a modest supply of culinary water below. We also cut an all-weather path down to the camp site, and covered it with gravel. Portable lavatory facilities were established in the camp area. As might be expected, about every time an event was schedule at "Camp Polly Turner," we got heavy rain, bogged-down vehicles, and water-logged campers but happy memories.[150]

In June 1972, the stake fathers and sons outing (commemorating the restoration of the Aaronic Priesthood) was held at Camp Polly Turner. Just two weeks later, a mothers and daughters outing was held under the direction of the Stake Aaronic Priesthood Committee. On July 10-16, the YWMIA scheduled their annual YWMIA Girl's Camp at Camp Turner. Forty-six of the fifty young women in attendance received their certification.

A traditional event much enjoyed by the High Priest Quorum was the annual social. Only one annual social was held, financed, in part, by contributions used to defray missionary support and other worthy projects. One feature of the social was the presentation of a suitable book to each high priest who completed a stake reading assignment. At the last stake conference of each year, President Taylor would charge all members to read one of the standard works (The Book of Mormon, for instance), and to notify him in writing. He would personally acknowledge their success with a letter. In addition, each high priest who completed this reading would receive a gift book signed by the quorum presidency (who were, of course, also the stake presidency).

The stake presidency was reorganized in 1971. Henry Heilesen accepted a position as Marketing Director of Mead Data Central, which took him out of the Cincinnati Area. He was succeeded by Lynn P. Wallace, a civil engineer with the Government who had recently arrived in Cincinnati. After a time, Fred Lundberg had a career opportunity elsewhere and left the area. Larry D. Bergen was called as a counselor in his place. Larry had come to Cincinnati as an engineer with The Procter & Gamble Company, and was legendary for his ability to fix anything, when he had time.

150.Ibid.

At the June 2nd conference in 1974, Lynn Wallace was released since he was moving from the area, and Larry D. Bergen was sustained as first counselor, and Wm. Budge Wallis as second counselor. Budge had come to Cincinnati to work for Proctor & Gamble, as well. He served as the first stake executive secretary and then as bishop of the Cincinnati First Ward.

Joe Banks Lengthens the Stake's Stride

Joseph W. Banks

When President Taylor was notified he would be released as stake president after serving nine and one-half years, he made sure everyone knew of the special stake conference where a new stake president would be sustained. Elder Gordon B. Hinkley was the visiting General Authority and it was a special treat to have a visit from a member of the Council of the Twelve. On conference day, June 1, 1975, a large crowd gathered to hear Elder Hinkley announce that Joseph William Banks had been called to serve as president of the Cincinnati Ohio Stake. Most of the congregation didn't know who he was. Joe Banks, as he liked to be called, had moved into the stake within the past year and was serving as the executive secretary in the Cincinnati First Ward. However, he was warmly received by the members of the stake and became well known for his compassion, his ability to speak on the spur of the moment, his straightforward counsel, and the intensity with which he approached every situation. He called Larry D. Bergen and Wm. Budge Wallis as his counselors. They both had been serving with President Taylor and provided continuity as President Banks knew very little about the stake.

The first week after he was set apart President Banks relates that as he was saying his prayers he saw the face of each high councilor and a voice told him about each one. This same vision came to him again that night. At the first high council meeting he called each high councilor by name and felt he knew them individually because of his dream.

President Bergen served a few months and then moved from the area and Darold Olson was called as second counselor. President Olson had been serving on the high council and had lived in the area a number of years so was well known throughout the stake.

During this time the Wilmington Branch was small and in need of strength. The branch president took a job out of the area, which required selection of a new presidency. President Banks discussed the situation with Presidents Wallis and Olson but they could not suggest a name for branch president. President Banks prayed that night before retiring and saw a name on the bed sheets as he was kneeling in prayer. The next day at his office he started to read his mail and across his desk was the same name. After reporting this experience to his counselors and with the approval of the High council, President Banks interviewed the man and called him to be the next branch president. The man was in his seventies, semiretired from a successful farming operation and had been spending the winter months in Florida for a number of years. When the call was extended his wife turned to him and told him that their trips to Florida would have to cease. He agreed and from that point on the small branch prospered.

The stake was in need of larger and better meeting facilities. The stake presidency and high council spent much time and effort in selecting building sites. Together they would walk through tall grass, weeds, and sometimes mud to check out potential plots. Much prayer and fasting took place to be guided by the Lord in selecting the proper plot of land. Land was found near Wilmington, Ohio, for a branch building. For many years the branch met in a small church building that had been built by the Quakers. Construction moved along quickly and it was dedicated by Royden G. Derrick the Sunday afternoon of the reorganization of the stake presidency, October 8, 1978.

The Cincinnati Fourth Ward was created from the Cincinnati West Branch on April 24, 1977. Merle Hargis was called as bishop with Donald Stoneking and Lonnie Smith as counselors. The organization took place in the Fairfield building as teh new ward had grown out of the Westwood town hall. The ward met in Northern Kentucky on Scott Street for a time and then moved to the Bosworth Place building.

The Cincinnati Fifth Ward was also created April 1977 from the Cincinnati First Ward and David Thompson was called as bishop with K. Nelson and Albert Steele as counselors. The Fifth Ward met in the Bosworth Place chapel with the Cincinnati First and Second Wards.

During President Banks' time as stake president the stake was moved from the Ohio Mission and made part of a newly created Louisville Kentucky mission. The first president was Reed Benson. He was a great speaker and the members always enjoyed hearing him. The stake was blessed to have Reed Benson's father, Ezra Taft Benson, president of the Quorum of the Twelve, visit several times during this period. During one visit as he was giving instructions to the stake presidency he asked why no stake center had been built. Even though a classroom had been converted into a stake president's office in the Norwood building Elder Benson encouraged effort to begin immediately to find property and build a stake meetinghouse.

The stake presidency and high council worked hard to find property. Many pieces of land were examined in the northeast suburbs of Cincinnati. Several different high councilors visited the owners of property on the corner of Snider and Cornell roads in Montgomery. Each time the family told these men they had no interest in selling the property. The more the committee searched the stronger they felt that this was the property the Lord wanted to be purchased. About six months after the last contact President Banks asked President Wallis to visit the property owners again and see if some progress could be made in interesting them in selling the land. President Wallis made careful preparations in developing a presentation complete with a color sketch of the proposed building. Stake leaders made it a matter of prayer that the way might be opened up to purchase the property. An appointment was made with Mr. Mills, owner of the property, and on the given evening President Wallis went to the quaint Swiss/German-looking home located in the trees behind the lot that seemed so well suited for a meetinghouse. Mr. Mills greeted President Wallis warmly and seemed to enjoy visiting.

Finally President Wallis introduced the subject of the property and explained the type of building the Church would build, how it would be used, the kind of meetings and gatherings that would take place, and how it would be maintained. He also showed him the color sketch of the proposed building. Mr. Mills responded by telling a story of their son who was going to school on the West Coast several years before and had a serious accident while hiking which required a long hospital stay. Mr. and Mrs. Mills went to San Francisco to visit their son. While riding a bus to the hospital two young ladies sat down by them, introduced themselves and found out what the Mills were doing. They explained they were missionaries for the Mormon Church and they would like to visit the Mills' son if it would be okay. The Mills gave their permission and later heard from their son that the missionaries visited him a number of times. This was a great comfort to the Mills as they had no friends or relatives in the area to visit their son. After Mr. Mills relayed this story he said any church that would care enough to visit a total stranger would be a good neighbor. He then explained that his wife had recently suffered a stroke. She was partially paralyzed and he wanted President Wallis to give her a blessing. President Wallis was happy to oblige and gave the blessing. Shortly thereafter an offer was made, accepted, and the property was purchased.

President Banks always looked forward to visiting the Cherry Fork Branch. This was a dependent branch formed from the Georgetown Ward in the Manchester, Cherry Fork, and West Union area. It was initially called the Manchester Branch as meetings were held in Harry Applegate's garage. Later the meetings were shifted to Elmer Rolf's garage in Cherry Fork. Although the garage had been carefully cleaned and painted it was not weatherproof. One cold winter Sunday the stake presidency visited the branch. The "stand" backed up to the closed garage doors, which were far from being airtight. A steady stream of ice cold air came through them onto the backs of the stake presidency. The congregation was seated toward the rear of the garage where the stove was located so they were quite warm. President Banks acted as if it were 72 degrees while Presidents Wallis and Olson were shivering and chilled to the bone.

The next meetingplace was the West Union firehouse. General meetings were held above the firetrucks in a second-floor room. Classes were held throughout the building including a small class around the back bumper of one of the firetrucks. The branch was blessed never to have a fire during Church services. Even under these circumstances the members were always friendly, happy to see each other, and radiated the spirit of the gospel.

While serving as stake president, President Banks received a call from Jack Clawson who was moving to the Batesville, Indiana, area to be president of Hill-Rom Manufacturing, a division of Hillenbrand Corporation. He had recently served as a stake president in Mississippi and wanted to know where he should attend church. He also expressed interest in starting a branch in the Batesville area. President Banks encouraged him to attend the Westwood Branch, which was then meeting in the Westwood Town Hall on the western side of Cincinnati until sufficient members could be gathered in the Batesville area for a small branch.

Four families began traveling from southeastern Indiana to the Cincinnati West Branch. President Banks found out that the southeastern section of Indiana was not claimed by any organized stake in Indiana or Kentucky. Since the people living in the area were oriented to Cincinnati for shopping and entertainment President Banks recommended to the Church leaders in Salt Lake City that the Cincinnati Stake should take responsibility for the area. In a short period of time there were sufficient numbers because of Church members moving into the area and locating members living in the region to establish a Batesville Branch. This took place in April 9, 1978. Jack Clawson was called as branch president with Lonnie Smith and Britt Lukens as counselors. This branch was not only a blessing to the Saints living in the area but the stake was blessed with leadership and input from the members living there. On September 24 of that same year, the Batesville Branch was made an independent branch.

President Banks focused on making the programs of the Church practical. For example the home teaching program was responsible for saving a sick child's life. About two in the morning President Banks was awakened by a phone call and asked by a man to help find someone who could donate a rare blood type for his daughter. The hospital did not have the blood and had been unable to find any. As it was a matter of life and death, President Banks called Presidents Wallis and Olson and they called the priesthood leaders in the stake. Quickly the home teachers called their families and a person was found with the needed blood type. The girl was saved. The father of the child was not a member at the time, but was soon baptized.

Almost as quickly as President Banks came to the Cincinnati area he left. General Motors Parts Division transferred President Banks to Jacksonville, Florida, in the fall of 1978. Elder Royden G. Derrick of the First Quorum of the Seventy officiated at the stake conference on October 8, 1978, when President Banks was released.

Robert D. Scott Prepares the Saints

Like Joe Banks, Robert D. Scott had only been living in the Cincinnati area a short time when he was called as president of the Cincinnati Ohio Stake on October 8, 1978. President Scott was transferred here by General Electric, having spent most of his career overseas in Australia and the Philippines. At the time of his call as stake president he was serving on the stake high council. Wm. Budge Wallis and George O. McVey were called as his counselors. President Scott characterized them as being "two of the finest counselors ever, very capable and fully able to be stake presidents themselves." This later became the case.

When Elder Derrick set President Scott apart he counseled him about four areas, "be out of debt, have clean finances, keep up-to-date records, and live a clean life. These will create a firm foundation for your leadership and without them your foundation will be undercut and you will fail." President Scott took this counsel to heart and set an example of industry and self-sufficiency. In his own life he was completely out of debt and he encouraged others to be also. He planted a huge garden and had most of his backyard

Robert D. Scott

devoted to fruit trees. His wife Doris was kept busy each summer preserving food in one form or another. He believed in and lived the principle of preparedness and he taught it to the stake.

Elder Derrick also promised President Scott the power of discernment. He had this gift and enjoyed it throughout his term as stake president. He was also given the gift of love that was felt by many throughout the stake. The day he gave his first talk to the stake he entered in his journal, "I told the people I needed their support and that I was not sure why the Lord chose me, but I would tell them why when I found out."

One of the first changes made after President Scott became stake president was the division of the Northern Kentucky Ward. J. Gordon Engar was called as the bishop of the Northern Kentucky First Ward.and Francis T. Mayo was called as bishop of the Northern Kentucky Second Ward.

**Budge Wallis, Henry Griffith, and George McVey
Break Ground for the Montgomery Stake Center**

It become clear within the first year of President Scott's term as stake president that he would help the stake raise money for and build a stake center on the property purchased in Montgomery. During this time wards and stakes were expected to raise a significant portion of the money needed to construct a building. The total cost of this new stake center, including the land, was $1.6 million and the stake was responsible for 30 percent of it. President Scott asked the stake members to sacrifice and each contribute a significant amount of money. He went to each ward and branch, and interviewed each active priesthood member. He encouraged them to commit to contribute a specific amount of money over the next year. As a family, the Scotts committed to contribute a sizable amount of money. Unknown to the members of the stake, they sold a choice piece of land they owned to keep this promise. President Scott felt if he was asking people to support the stake building fund his family had to make a real sacrifice first.

Groundbreaking for the new stake center was September 6, 1980. This was a Saturday and the regional representative, Henry Griffith presided. President Scott did not attend because of the sudden death of his grandchild in New York state. When Presidents Wallis and McVey arrived for the groundbreaking they were shocked to see that a bulldozer had already "broken ground" and had cleared off a large section of the property. The program went ahead as though the land was undisturbed and stake and ward leaders turned over dirt with gold-painted shovels at the appropriate time. The stake had been organized for well over twenty years without a stake center. President Scott was driven and consumed with the desire to get the building built. His leadership was key in making this happen.   According to his wife Doris, he had never worked so hard at a Church calling in his life.

President Scott used a success formula Elder Franklin D. Richards gave him at the airport as he was leaving from a stake conference visit in Cincinnati in 1980. This was his success formula for business and Church. He said, "have a plan, keep it simple, be strong yourself in all areas (physically, mentally, and spiritually), and learn to pace yourself." President Scott was successful in helping the stake not only raise but greatly exceed the funds needed to build the stake center. At the same time the Cincinnati Stake was one of the first stakes to pay their assessment for a new temple being built in the Chicago area.

The members throughout the stake came to help paint, landscape, and clean the building as it was being finished. It was not hard to get volunteers, as members of the stake were so excited and proud to have such a large and beautiful Church building in the area.

A few months before the first meetings were held in the new stake center President Scott's employer transferred him to Malaysia. He and his family moved immediately. He was released as stake president three years to the day after he was called. A month later, on November 14, 1981, the Cincinnati, Ohio, stake center was dedicated, thus fulfilling President Scott's dream.

Wm. Budge Wallis Divides the Stake

Wm. Budge Wallis was sustained and set apart as stake president of the Cincinnati Ohio Stake by Elder David B. Haight of the Council of the Twelve on October 8, 1981. President Wallis had served over the past seven years as a counselor to the last three stake presidents. John Taylor wrote of him saying: "He was a grand fellow, . . . He was a natural to serve as a counselor, and I knew that one day he would be stake president, as indeed he was, and a splendid one."[151] George McVey was called as first counselor and

---

151. John A. Taylor, personal history

Wm. Budge Wallis

Darold Olson, who was bishop of the Cincinnati Third Ward was called as second counselor.

Elder Haight seemed to enjoy his visit to Cincinnati and while here President Wallis asked if he would dedicate the new stake center. The building was completed in September l981 and several meetings had already been held in it. Elder Haight said he would be delighted to come back. Elder Haight made some major changes in his schedule and returned on November l4, l981, and dedicated the new stake center. Mr. Mills, previous owner of the land, was present and seemed to enjoy the meeting and his new neighbors.

Several events were held before the dedication to increase awareness of the Church in the community. A breakfast was held in the new stake center for clergy from the denominations in the surrounding communities.   The breakfast was prepared and served by the Relief Society and after a short program member guides took small groups through the building and not only showed the facility but explained the basic beliefs of the Church. On the whole the clergy members were favorably impressed and positive in their comments about the building and the Church.   An open house was held for members and their friends and the public for several days. Also a number of newspaper articles were published about the new stake center. Brent Anderson, a high councilor, was on a local radio talk show answering questions about the Church. An original musical, "Families Are Forever," written by Ronald McCroby, was performed during an open house and many friends attended. All of this attention and notice went a long way to help bring the Church out of obscurity in the area.

In early l983 property was found near Batesville, Indiana, for a branch building. The branch had been meeting for several years in an old cinder-block warehouse near Sunman, Indiana. The branch had furnished the building with carpeted floor, old pews from a recently remodeled church building, and old folding chairs. The building was extremely cold in the winter and hot in the summer. The branch members were anxious to have a building of their own. On April 24, l983, a groundbreaking ceremony was held. The weather was very cold but the Spirit was strong. Many turned out to witness the event. The Batesville Indiana Branch meetinghouse was constructed during l983 and l984.   On November l8, l984, the building was dedicated by President Wallis. The branch had grown from several families five years before to a membership of l60. There was a wonderful spirit of unity in the branch and between those who had moved in to work for Hillenbrand Industries, those who had joined the Church, and those who had been activated.

On June 3, 1984 the Cincinnati Sixth Ward was organized from portions of the Cincinnati Second and Fifth Wards as well as the Hamilton Ward. The creation of this ward increased the number of units in the stake to twelve with three wards meeting in the new stake center on Cornel Road.

The members in the two Northern Kentucky Wards experienced slow but steady growth during the l980s. Their building, located on Scott Street in Covington, was small, located in an inconvenient area to most of the membership, and parking was a nightmare. The building had been remodeled several times yet was still inadequate. In December l984, a 3.5-acre piece of land was purchased on Buttermilk Pike in Lakeside Park, Kentucky. This property was acquired after about eight years of active searching. It was to be the location of a new building for the two Northern Kentucky wards. The stake presidency had called numerous land search committees and had looked at many pieces of property, but time and time again the land being considered was rejected. The stake presidency was confident the Lakeside Park property was the place the Lord wanted a building to be built and discussed its use as a future stake center that would be needed some day..

**The new Cincinnati and Cincinnati North Stake Presidencies
(Elder James Campbell, Page Busken, George McVey, Budge Wallis,
Brent Sommers, Darold Olson, and Rex Reeve, seated;
Francis Mayo was not present)**

After much study and prayer it was felt that a recommendation should be made to divide the stake on a north-south basis as the stake had grown large enough (twelve units) to support two stakes. This took place on March 17, 1985, under the direction of Elder Rex C. Reeve Sr. of the Council of Seventy and Elder James Campbell, regional representative. George O. McVey was sustained as president of the Cincinnati Ohio Stake with Francis T. Mayo as first counselor and D. Page Busken as second counselor. President Wallis was sustained as president of the new Cincinnati Ohio North Stake with President Darold Olson as first counselor and Brent Somers as second counselor. Each stake consisted of six units. The Cincinnati Stake included Cincinnati First, Fourth, and Fifth wards, Northern Kentucky First and Second wards and the Batesville Indiana Branch. The Cincinnati North Stake included Cincinnati Second, Third, and Sixth wards, Hamilton Ward, Georgetown Ward, and Wilmington Branch. Where one stake existed on November 23, 1958, four stakes were functioning in 1985. In addition to the two Cincinnati stakes, the Dayton area, which was part of the original Cincinnati Stake, now had two stakes, and all were well-poised for even greater growth in the near future.

Epilogue

The original scope of this history was to research and gather events connected with the establishment and growth of the Mormon Church in the Cincinnati area up to the division of the Cincinnati Stake in 1985. This has been accomplished, but it has taken years longer than expected, and much has happened in the growth of the Church since 1985.

New branches have been formed in Oxford, Lawrenceburg, and Adams County as well as new wards in Milford, West Chester, Northern Kentucky, and Anderson township. President Wallis was released as president of the Cincinnati North Stake in August 1990 with Brent Sommers serving until August 1995 and then George Rahlf succeeding him. In the Cincinnati Stake, President McVey served until 1992 and was followed by Neil Hahl. New buildings have been built and the older ones have been remodeled and expanded. In addition each ward and branch have had many important and faith promoting experiences that are not documented here.

We regret that we cannot include these important events in this history but take heart that other histories will follow and that there is yet much more to be said and written about the Church of Jesus Christ of Latter-day Saints in the Cincinnati area. We have a rich heritage here and a promising future.

References

Aaron, Daniel. *Cincinnati, Queen City of the West, 1819-1838.* Columbus, Ohio: Ohio State University Press, 1992.

Allen, James B., and Glen M. Leonard. *The Story of the Latter-day Saints.* Salt Lake City, Utah: Deseret Book Company, 1976.

Anderson, Charles V. *Twenty-Three Years in Cincinnati.* Salt Lake City, Utah: Self-published.

Backman, Milton V., Jr., ed. *Regional Studies in Latter-day Saint History: Ohio.* Provo, Utah: Department of Church History and Doctrine, 1990.

Barnes, Lorenzo Dow. Diary, 2 vols., Church Archives, Historical Department, Church of Jesus Christ of Latter-day Saints, Salt Lake City, Utah.

Bitton, Davis. "Kirtland as a Center of Missionary Activity, 1830-1838," *BYU Studies* 11 (Summer 1971):497-516.

Bushman, Richard. *Joseph Smith and the Beginnings of Mormonism.* Urbana and Chicago: University of Illinois Press, 1984.

Clark, James R., ed. *Messages of the First Presidency of The Church of Jesus Christ of Latter-day Saints [1833-1951].* 6 vols. Salt Lake City, Utah: Bookcraft, 1965-1975.

Conference Reports of The Church of Jesus Christ of Latter-day Saints. Salt Lake City: The Church of Jesus Christ of Latter-day Saints, 1880, 1897-1970.

Coray, Howard. *Howard Coray Journal.* Typescript, Brigham Young University Archives and Manuscripts, Provo, Utah.

Cowley, Matthias F. W*ilford Woodruff: Fourth President of The Church of Jesus Christ of Latter-day Saints—History of His Life and Labors As Recorded in His Daily Journals.* Salt Lake City, Utah: Deseret News, 1909.

Crawley, Peter. "A Bibliography of the Church of Jesus Christ of Latter-day Saints in New York, Ohio, and Missouri" *BYU Studies*, 12 (Summer 1972): 465-538.

Crawley, Peter. "The Constitution of the State of Deseret" *BYU Studies*, 29 (Fall 1989), 7-20.

The Doctrine and Covenants of The Church of Jesus Christ of Latter-day Saints. Salt Lake City,Utah: The Church of Jesus Christ of Latter-day Saints, 1981.

Ellwood, Robert. *The Autobiography of Robert Ellwood*, Mormon Biographical Sketches Collection (ca. 1900-1975).

England, Breck. *The Life and Thought of Orson Pratt.* Salt Lake City, Utah: University of Utah Press, 1985.

The Evening and The Morning Star. Edited by William W. Phelps and Oliver Cowdery. 2 vols. Independence, Missouri, and Kirtland, Ohio: June 1832 to September 1834.

Garrett, H. Dean., ed. *Regional Studies in Latter-day Saint History: Illinois.* Provo, Utah: Department of Church History and Doctrine, 1995.

Greene, John P. *Facts Relative to the Expulsion of the Mormons or Latter Day Saints, from the State of Missouri, under the "Exterminating Order." by John P. Greene, an Authorized Representative of the Mormons.* Cincinnati, Ohio: R.P. Brooks, 1839.

Harlow, Alvin F. *The Serene Cincinnatians.* New York: E.P. Dutton & Co., 1950.

Hayden, A.S. *Early History of the Disciples in the Western Reserve, Ohio.* Cincinnati, Ohio: Chase and Hall, 1875; reprinted, New York: Arno Press and the New York Times, 1972.

Hurley, Daniel. *Cincinnati: The Queen City.* Bicentennial ed. Cincinnati, Ohio: Cincinnati Historical Society, 1988.

Jenson, Andrew. *Encyclopedic History of The Church of Jesus Christ of Latter-day Saints.* Salt Lake City, Utah: Deseret News Publishing Company, 1941.

Jenson, Andrew. *Latter-day Saint Biographical Encyclopedia: A Compilation of Biographical Sketches of Prominent Men and Women in the Church of Jesus Christ of Latter-day Saints.* 4 vols. Salt Lake City, Utah. A. Jenson History Company and Deseret News, 1901-36.

Jessee, Dean C. "Joseph Smith's 19 July 1840 Discourse," *BYU Studies*, 19 (Spring 1979): 390.

Johnson, Clark V. , ed., *Mormon Redress Petitions: Documents of the 1833–1838 Missouri Conflic*t. Salt Lake City, Utah: Bookcraft, Inc., 1992.

Journal History of the Church of Jesus Christ of Latter-day Saints. 16 February 1835, Church Archives, Historical Department, Church of Jesus Christ of Latter-day Saints, Salt Lake City, Utah.

Kelsey, Eli B. Journal, Church Archives, Historical Department, Church of Jesus Christ of Latter-day Saints, Salt Lake City, Utah.

The Latter Day Saints' Messenger and Advocate. Edited by Oliver Cowdery, et al. 3 vols. Kirtland, Ohio: F. G. Williams & Co., et al., October 1834 to August 1837.

Pettegrew, David. Journal, holograph copy, Brigham Young University Special Collections, Provo, Utah.

Pratt, Parley P. *The Autobiography of Parley Parker Pratt, One of the Twelve Apostles of the Church of Jesus Christ of Latter-day Saints, Embracing His Life, Ministry and Travels, With Extracts, in Prose and Verse, from his Miscellaneous Writings.* Salt Lake City: Deseret Book Company, 1985.

Reeves, Ota , ed. "Historical Highlights of the Cincinnati Stake," Church Archives. 1962.

The Return. Edited by Ebenezer Robinson. 3 vols. Davis City, Iowa, 1888-1890.

Roberts, B.H. *Comprehensive History of The Church of Jesus Christ of Latter-day Saints.* 6 vols. 1930. Reprint. Orem, Utah: Sonos Publishing Inc., 1991.

Skinner, Andrew C. "John C. Bennett: For Prophet or Profit?" In *Regional Studies--Illinois*, H. Dean Garrett, ed. Provo, Utah: Department of Church History and Doctrine, Brigham Young University, 1995.

Smith, Joseph, Jr. *History of The Church of Jesus Christ of Latter-day Saints.* Edited by B.H. Roberts. 2d ed., rev. 7 vols. Salt Lake City, Utah: Deseret Book, 1980.

Smith, Lucy Mack. *History of Joseph Smith, By His Mother, Lucy Mack Smith.* Edited by Preston Nibley. Salt Lake City: Bookcraft, 1954.

Snow, Eliza R. *Biography and Family Record of Lorenzo Snow.* Salt Lake City, Utah: Deseret News Company, 1884.

Sutton, Walter. *The Western Book Trade: Cincinnati as a Nineteenth-Century Publishing and Book-trade Center.* Columbus, Ohio: Ohio State University Press, 1961.

Tate, Charles D. Jr. "Howard and Martha Jane Knowlton Coray of Nauvoo," *Regional Studies--Illinois*, Edited by H. Dean Garrett. Provo, Utah: Department of Church History and Doctrine, Brigham Young University, 1995.

Times and Seasons. Edited by Ebenezer Robinson, et al. 6 vols. Commerce, Illinois, and Nauvoo, Illinois, 1839-1846 (131 issues).

Wallis, James H. , Diary, Cincinnati Ohio, 31 January, 1935-16 February, 1935. In possession of Gloria Wallis Rytting.

Watkins, William. *Autobiography of William Lampard Watkins*, typescript, Brigham Young University Special Collections, Provo, Utah.

Watson, Elden J., ed. *The Orson Pratt Journals.* Salt Lake City, Utah: E.J. Watson, 1975.

Index

A

Abshire, Virginia 70
Adams, George J. 25, 37
Adams, W.J. 52
Affleck, Stephen B. 92
All-Church Basketball Tournament champions 93
Allred, Isaac 41
An Appeal to the American People 35
Anderson, Charles V. 50
Anderson, Christine 50, 52
Andrus, Hyrum 89
Applegate, Harry 99

B

Bair, John 20
Bang, Christian Jr. 66
Bang, Christian, Sr. 53, 58
Bang, Henry 66
Bang, Paul 66, 70, 88, 93
Bang, Rosa 52
Bang, Samuel 68
Bang, Victor 68, 70
Banks, Joe 97
Banks, John 41
Barnes, Lorenzo D. 5
Barrett, Ivan J. 89
Basset, Charles H. 40
Batavia, Ohio 10
Batesville Branch 100, 103
Baum, Ronald C. 92
Bellefontaine Branch 87, 94
Bellevue, Kentucky 55
Bennet, Michael 87
Bennett, John C. 40
Bennett, Samuel 19, 23
Benson, Reed 98
Bent, Samuel 11
Bergen, Larry D. 96
Berry, Joel M. 42
Bishop, Gladden 40
Black, John C. 92
Blackham, Andus Udell 77
Blackwelder, Clayton 68

Blackwelder, Daniel A. 68
Blackwelder, Julius 71, 78, 87
Book of Commandments 28
Book of Mormon 28
Boone County, Kentucky 16
Bosworth Place chapel 79
Boulter, Lynn James 90
Brigham Young Academy 17
Brigham Young University 89
Broman, Edward R. 77
Brooks, Howard C. 95
Brookville, Indiana 5
Browman, Edward J. 80
Brown, Samuel 19
Bryson, Vern 82
Burch, Daniel 23
Burch, James 19
Burton, Carl C. 81
Busken, D. Page 104
Butt, W.F. 46
Buttermilk Pike chapel 103

C

Cahall, Dorothy 70
Cahall, O. Vernon 64, 66, 87, 91
Callis, Charles A. 50, 60
Camp Polly Turner 96
Campbell County, Kentucky 7
Campbell house 79
Campbell, Thomas 3
Campbellites 3
Cardon, Joseph E. 47
Carter, Simeon 22
Carthage, Ohio 9
Central Parkway YMCA 66
Chapin, Crafton Grant 92
Chapin, Laverne 70
Chapin, Raymond 64, 87
Cherry Fork Branch 99
Cincinnati Commercial 38
Cincinnati Fifth Ward 98
Cincinnati Fourth Ward 98
Cincinnati North Stake 104

Cincinnati Republican 40
Cincinnati Second Ward, 88
Cincinnati Sixth Ward 103
Cincinnati Stake 83, 84
Cincinnati Third Ward 92
Cincinnati West Branch 95
Clark Riley G., Jr. 47
Clark, Riley Garner 19
Clawson, Jack 100
Clawson, Rudger 51, 62
Clive, Clifford 88
Cloud, George N. 87
Coe, Joseph 3
Collins, John 11
Connersville Branch 94
Cook, Alva May 68
Coray, Howard 16
Corbin, Dewitt T. 71, 74
Cornell Road chapel 98, 102
Cottle, Thomas 47
Covington chapel 86
Covington, Kentucky 5, 16, 55
Cowdery, Oliver 3
Cowley, Mathias F. 47
Cox, Elmer 71, 74
Crippin, John W. 20, 26
Crockett, Ezra D. 47
Culbertson, Robert 19
Cummingsville 8

D

Daily Sun, The 37
David, D.J. 46
Davidson, David J. 47
Davis, David J. 46
Dayton Stake, creation of 94
Dayton Ward 94
Dayton, Kentucky 55
Dayton, Ohio 19, 23, 26, 63
Dearborn County, Indiana 13, 15
Democratic Committee of Cincinnati 33
DeRossier, Theodore A. 80
Dickore, Marie 43, 92
Dixon, Charles E. 88
Doughty, Edward 11
Druck, Robert 68
Dykes, George P. 27

E

Ellwood, Robert 42
Engar, Gordon 101
Erekson, John B. 46, 47
Ethington, Gilbert B. 68
Evans, T. Blair 82, 83
Evening and Morning Star, The 28

F

Fairborn chapel 86
Fairborn Ward 94
Fish, Joseph Smith 50
Fish, Melvin 93
Fish, Merlin K. 68, 80, 87, 88
Fish, Merlin V. 94
Fish, Stanley L. 70, 76, 81, 92
Fletcher, Robert 58
Forbes, Homer R. 88
Frontier Guardian 28
Ft. Thomas, Kentucky 55
Fulton, Ohio 8

G

Genealogical library 92
Georgetown chapel 86
Georgetown Ward, creation of 87
Georgetown, Kentucky 25
Gibby, Irvin 71
Gilbert, Algernon S. 3
Gilliam, A.B. 58, 65, 78
Gilliam, Pat 71
Ginn, Robert 92
Gleason and Shepherd, printers 29
Gloss, Fred 51
Gooch, John 28
Goshen, Alma Clair 68
Grange, Merlene 68
Grant, Heber J. 61
Grant, Joshua 20
Greene, John P. 33

H

Hale, Howard H. 47
Hamby, Chester 68
Hamby, Everett 68
Hamilton Branch 78
Hamilton, Curtis L. 88
Hanks, John 71
Hanks, Marion D. 68, 86
Hansen, A.K. 47
Harbreck, Anna 52
Hargis, Merle 98
Harkness, Randy 93
Harris, Martin 3
Harrison, Ohio 6
Haslam, George 70
Haun's Mill Massacre 36
Haymond, Creed 75
Heaton, Iris 68
Heilsesen, Henry 91
Heitzmann, Bernita 52
Higbee, A.V.H. 11
Higbee, Elias 12
Higbee, Elmira 11
Higbee, Isaac, Jr. 12, 15

Higbee, Isaac, Sr. 11
Higbee, James C. 11
Higbee, John S. 12
Higbee, Sophia 12
Hill, George B. 82
Hinckley, Bryant S. 49
Hintze, Alan 78
Hope, Len and Mary 58
Hyde, Orson 23, 28, 34

J
Jensen, James P. 70
Johnson, Henry Mitchell 19

K
Katterhenry, E.H. 42
Keller, Sarah 52
Kelsey, Eli B. 27
Ketch, Louis A. 46
Kettering Ward 90, 94
Kimball, Heber C. 24
Kirkham, Oscar A. 67
Knott, Marie 95
Knott, Thomas L. 87, 95
Knowlton, Martha Jane 16
Knowlton, Sidney 16

L
Lamoreaux, A.L. 23
Latonia, Kentucky 55
Lee, Harold B. 87
Lewistown, Ohio 12
Licking River 19
Louisville Kentucky Mission 98
Lowe, Carma 79
Lowe, Paul E. 82, 83
Ludlow, Kentucky 55
Lukens, Britt 100
Lundberg, Enfred J. 92
Lundquist, Roy E. 78, 81, 90
Lyman, Amasa 25
Lyman, Francis M. 47
Lyman, Richard R. 67

M
Mason, Gus 64, 76
Mason, Ohio 19
Massie, Ross 92
Mauss, Michael 46, 47
Mayhew, Walter F. 46, 47
Mayo, Francis T. 101, 104
McBride, Marjorie 68
McCroby, Ronald 103
McCullum, Cornelius 11
McKay, David O. 60
McPhie, Joseph M. 94
McVey, George O. 104

McVey, George O. 100, 102
Meadows, Margie Evelyn 80
Meier, Robert 64
Merryweather, Frederick 27
Middle States Mission 47
Middletown Branch 78
Middletown chapel 86
Middletown Ward 90, 94
Milford, Ohio 10
Mill Creek, Ohio 19
Mormon Battalion 15, 19
Moroni 42
Mortenson, James 82
Muir, Leo J. 67
Mulberry, Ohio 10
Munsen, Lloyd M. 88
Murdock, John 5
Muttings, Sister 8

N
Nauvoo angel 42
Nauvoo Legion 15
Nelson, K. 98
New Trenton, Indiana 26
Newport, Kentucky 55
Newtown, Ohio 10
Nichols, Paul 71
Northern Kentucky Branch 78
Northern States Mission 46

O
Olson, Darold 97, 103
Orchard Street chapel 55, 66

P
Page, John E. 10, 16, 23, 24
Partridge, Edward 3
Paul, J.P. 52
Peck, Louise Rae 68
Perintown, Ohio 10
Peterson, Mark E. 83
Peterson, Ziba 3
Pettegrew, David 13, 26
Pettegrew, Elizabeth 13
Pettit, Richard 27
Phelps, W.W. 3, 28
Piqua Branch 94
Plummer, Carl 92
Plummer, Harriet 92
Polygamy 39
Pond, Noah S. 55, 61
Pratt, Orson 5, 24
Pratt, Parley P. 3
Pratt, William Dickinson 5
Prickett family 49
Pugh, Elder 27

R

Ratliff, James A. 87
Rebert, Janice 71
Reeve, Rex C. 104
Reichardt, P. Winton 87
Reynolds, George 48
Rich, Ben E. 47
Richards, LeGrand 83
Richards, Lorin L. 81
Richards, Stephen L. 54
Rigdon, Sidney 3
Robbins, Lewis 5
Robinson, Ebenezer 28
Robinson, George W. 34
Rolf, Elmer 99
Rolph, Charles A. 90
Romney, George S. 62
Russell, Harry J. 87
Ryan, Alma 94

S

Salem Evangelical Reform Church 42
Scott, Gerald L. 91
Scott, Robert D. 100
Scott, Walter 3, 9
Shelbyville, Indiana 5
Sidney Rigdon 35
Sink, Jerry 93
Smith, Don Carlos 28
Smith, Emma 3, 27
Smith, Felice Swain 68
Smith, George A. 16, 24
Smith, Joseph 3, 16, 28
Smith, Lonnie 98, 100
Smith, Lucy Mack 17
Snow, Lorenzo 25
Somers, Brent 104
South Ohio District 76
Southern States Mission 49
Spencer, Orson 41
Spenser, Herbert B. 90
Springdale, Ohio 23
Springfield chapel 86
Springfield Ward 88, 94
Standing, Joseph 62
Stearns and Shepherd, printers 29
Steele, Albert 98
Stephen, Adeline Louise 68
Stewart, James G. 69
Stoneking, Donald 98
Strang, James 40
Sugar Creek, Indiana 5
Switzerland County, Indiana 19
Sydney Branch 87

T

Taylor, Adeline 70
Taylor, John A. 83, 84, 91
Taylor, John H. 60
Taylor, Milton 76
Terre Haute, Indiana 5
Thieler, Louis 80
Thompson, David 98
Times and Seasons 28
Tolman, Myrtle 68
Turley, Edward F. 47

V

Vernon. Leo P. 94
Victory Parkway chapel 71

W

Walker, Stephen 41
Wallace, Lynn 96
Wallis, James H. 62
Wallis, Wm. Budge 62, 97, 100, 102
Wardwell, Randy 93
Warren County, Ohio 23
Washington Court House, Ohio 19
Washington DC temple 92
Watkins, William 25
Waynesville, Ohio 19, 26
Western Messenger 35
Westwood Branch 99
Wheeler, Marion 68
Whitmer, Peter 2, 3
Whitney, Orson F. 56
Wight, Lyman 4, 24
Wilmington Branch 88, 97
Wilson, Calves 4
Wilson, Joseph E., Jr. 47
Winn, Noel E. 95
Wolford, Leon 90
Woodlawn, Kentucky 55
Woodruff, Wilford 24, 25
Word of Wisdom 26

Y

Y.M.C.A 55
Young, Brigham 24, 38
Young, Noah 47

Z

Zachrison, John 87